P9-CKU-299

NOTES & JOURNAL

NOTES AND JOURNAL
OF
TRAVEL IN EUROPE
1804–1805

BY

WASHINGTON IRVING

With an Introduction by William P. Trent and Title-page and Illustrations in Aquatint Designed and Engraved by Rudolph Ruzicka

IN THREE VOLUMES

VOLUME I

New York
THE GROLIER CLUB

1921

Republished 1971
Scholarly Press, Inc., 22929 Industrial Drive East
St. Clair Shores, Michigan 48080

Library of Congress Catalog Card Number: 70-107176
ISBN 0-403-00385-7

CONTENTS

OF FIRST VOLUME

INTRODUCTION

THE Notes of travel and the Journal founded upon them, here for the first time reproduced faithfully and in considerable fullness, have been known in outline and in fragments for about two generations, that is, since the appearance of the initial volume of *The Life and Letters of Washington Irving*, edited by his nephew Pierre. The nearly sixty years that have intervened, if they have not precisely increased the fame of "America's first author," have at least solidified and firmly established it; hence the publication of these memorials of Irving's earliest visit to that Old World which he was later to interpret so sympathetically to the New, may be justified on the ground that it is interesting and useful to read and study materials that throw additional light upon the formative years of a writer who has become one of his country's classics, nay more, who has won for himself a not undistinguished position among the authors of the world.

Yet, when one lays great emphasis upon the biographical or autobiographical value of a book, does not one run the risk of incurring the suspicion that one is not so very sure of its strictly literary value? Might we not with some fairness define a good book as one that would attract, or ought to attract, an intelligent reader, even if he made its acquaintance in a copy that had lost its title-page? We need not attempt to answer these questions, but they have their bearing on the present publication. If I am not mistaken, this Journal and these Notes of more than a century ago would be both interesting and valuable, even if we had no inkling of the identity of their author. If, with Irving's name obliterated, they had been found in a mass of rubbish by a person unaccustomed to conduct literary investigations and unacquainted with the fact that the famous writer travelled in Europe early in the nineteenth century, the finder, if he had read the rescued manuscripts carefully, would surely have been lacking in acumen if he had failed to perceive that they were the records of a young traveller of engaging disposition, keen intelligence, kindly humor, fresh, unjaded sympathies, and lively patriotism — in short, of a voyager of a by-gone day who, despite occasional exhibitions of immaturity and inexperience, was much above the ordinary. To ask whether this lucky finder would have offered his treasure to the Grolier Club for publication, and whether the Club, in terms of stereotyped courtesy, would have "embraced the opportunity" to give the manuscripts to the world of book lovers, is to inquire too curiously. I may remark, however, that if the supposititious finder had taken the trouble to make a cursory examination of the volumes of travels devoted to the France and Italy of the period of his manuscripts, he would probably have come to the conclusion that his discovery should see the light, if only that an addition might be made to the few books of this category that do not weary modern readers through their jejuneness.[1]

Here, I regret to say, another question obtrudes itself. Is not this young man's Journal distinguished in its lack of stiltedness from the mass of the conventional travel literature of its day because its writer was that Washington Irving who was later so famous that a British lady took occasion to announce, with becoming complacence, that General George Washington was the author of *The Sketch Book*? But when one begins to ask questions of this sort, one never knows when to stop. Let us there-

[1] The travel literature of the period was not inconsiderable in quantity, and some of it was carefully read by Irving in connection with his tour. The chief travellers he quotes are three in number, and they rank among the best writers of their kind during the last quarter of the eighteenth century. They are Patrick Brydone (1736-1818), Henry Swinburne (1743-1803), and the better known physician-author John Moore (1729-1802), called "Zeluco Moore" from the name of his once famous novel. The *Tour through Sicily and Malta* (1773) of the first was very popular, and one suspects that Irving, although he thought it unreliable, used it occasionally to refresh his

fore ask and attempt to answer a question of a different sort—What were Irving's character and circumstances when he began the Journal we are soon to follow?

On July 1, 1804, the day he wrote the first words in the small blank book selected to contain the initial records of his journey, Irving, who was born in New York City on April 3, 1783, was almost twenty-one years and three months old. He had landed at Bordeaux the day before, after a continuous voyage of forty-two days, thus defeating the now famous prediction of the ship's captain, made as the consumptive passenger was helped up the side of the vessel at New York, "There 's a chap who will go overboard before we get across." Worthy Captain Shaler doubtless knew nothing of the wiriness of the blended Scotch and English stocks from which the invalid sprang, and equally little of the spiritual, mental, and physical elasticity

memory when referring to and quoting the classics for the benefit of his American kinsfolk. He probably read also Swinburne's *Travels in the Two Sicilies* (1783, 1785) and Moore's *View of Society and Manners in Italy* (1781), to which he certainly added the latter's *View of Society and Manners in France, Switzerland, and Germany* (1779). Undoubtedly he could not and did not read one of the most intelligent but outwardly most unattractive books of the period, *Briefe aus der Hauptstadt und dem Innern Frankreichs*, by Dr. F. J. L. Meyer, canon in Hamburg (Tübingen, 1802).

of the youth himself. Perhaps, if he had known something of Irving's experiences in Canada the summer before, with the Hoffmans, the Ogdens, and — more especially — the Indians, he might have prophesied less confidently. At any rate, we may be sure he was glad when he saw the youngster, after a slight attack of seasickness and despite the fever that troubled him at night, displaying such an interest in seamanship that he became "quite expert at climbing to the mast-head and going out on the main topsail yard." An invalid who did not go overboard doing that was not likely to go overboard in the more gruesomely prepared manner predicted by the captain. In some way or other the active youth in "round jacket and loose trowsers" was spared to become one of the best-beloved of authors. Throughout the Journal we find scarcely an intimation of invalidism, save such as may lurk in the references to the salubrity of places visited, and we are not surprised when the seasoned sailor, no longer subject even to slight attacks of seasickness, dwells with perhaps more than necessary self-satisfaction upon the ravages made by that dire ailment on fellow passengers subsequently observed in the midst of their encounters with the untrustworthy waves of the Mediterranean.

Irving's pranks on the masts and yards, which

might not have been undertaken on any but "a lady's voyage," reveal the fact that he was still a boy, and they carry us back to surreptitious climbing exploits of his early years. They help also to explain the fact that the Journal frequently shows signs of weariness over pictures and statues and gives much evidence of a predilection for movement and for genial personal intercourse. More important still, they seem to indicate a certain mobility of temperament inherited, it would appear, rather from the English mother than from the somewhat rigid Scotch father. The Irving we learn to know from the Journal and from the home-sent letters based on that is not, so far as we can judge, a morbid invalid concerned with the state of his health and his soul; he is instead the same Irving who was confirmed in Trinity Church by stealth, who soon developed a fondness for the theatre gratified often without his father's knowledge — and to be gratified in Europe to an extent which the brother standing to him as a father can scarcely have relished — who delighted in reading heroic poetry and narratives of adventure, who soon tried his own pen at verses, plays, and essays, who received instruction in music and stole lessons in dancing — balls play their part in the Journal — who, in short, accommodated himself as best he could to the restricted and provincial, though not markedly repressive, environment of his boyhood and youth. Quite as clearly he is the Irving who obtained a rather poor schooling, who, for reasons he never understood, was not entered at Columbia College, as two of his brothers had been, who became enamoured of the scenery and legends of the Hudson — perhaps as yet with no premonitions of *Rip Van Winkle* and *The Legend of Sleepy Hollow* — who displayed little aptitude for the law, but much for summer journeys into the less settled parts of New York State, who formed warm friendships, one of which was destined to lead to the romantic, frustrated attachment that illustrates so touchingly the exquisite tenderness and beauty of character of the mellowest of American writers.

These glimpses of the past of the young man we are to accompany on his journeys would be sufficient, perhaps, for our purposes were it not for one important omission. The Journal, after all allowances have been made for haste and for the changes that a century has brought to English spelling and diction, is obviously the work of a youthful gentleman not carefully trained in orthography, punctuation, and some of the more mechanical features of style, but it is just as obviously the work of a neophyte man of letters, well read for his years and endowed with remarkable ease and felicity of expression. This is just what we should expect of a youth, who, despite his slight schooling and lack of application to the law, had already attained some distinction as a budding author. The writer of this Journal had begun nearly two years before, in the *Morning Chronicle* edited by his brother, Peter Irving, the publication of the Addisonian essays of "Jonathan Oldstyle." They were admired and copied, American literature being then in its infancy, and they brought their young author — he was not twenty — a visit and literary proposals that must have flattered him greatly, coming as they did from a writer then much thought of, now somewhat unduly neglected, our first novelist of importance, Charles Brockden Brown. Irving would not contribute to Brown's magazine, but his Journal and his letters show that a marked aptitude for writing lay in the diarist who in a few years was to be known as the author of *Salmagundi* and of *Knickerbocker's History of New York.* What is more, — for the faculty of undertaking, carrying on, and making interesting a journal of travels is not one possessed by the majority of writers, or even of essayists,— this literary apprentice had kept a journal of his trip to Ogdensburg made during the summer that preceded his voyage to Europe.

These facts, as well as some notion of the looseness of English orthography, even after the Great Lexicographer had been in his grave thirty years, and some sympathetic comprehension of the manners, style, and general point of view of the late eighteenth century, must be in our minds if we are to obtain to the full the pleasure this long withheld Journal is capable of affording; but its freshness, sincerity, and general fluency ought, one would think, to make it attractive even to persons not specially interested in Irving or in the century in which he was born. If any reader, exasperated by modern spelling reformers, should find his pleasure marred by the faithful reproduction of the orthography of the Journal, we may comfort him by the assurance that a perusal of the private correspondence of people of quality in the reign of Queen Anne will convince him that, even in Irving's hands, English spelling was a more sacrosanct thing than it had been a hundred years before. But let us turn to the traveller's Journal, which is surely more important than his spelling or even his grammar, dear though such high mysteries are to the votaries of Webster and of Lindley Murray.

The opening of the Journal takes the form of a letter to his much older brother William, on whom most of the expenses of the tour were to fall. Washington had landed in Bordeaux — which he first wrote in its eighteenth century spelling, *Bourdeaux* — on the preceding day, the thirtieth of June. After waiting a week, during which he collected his thoughts and sated his eyes and ears with novel sights and sounds, he began a second instalment, really another letter, though not definitely addressed. Gradually the instalments become more frequent, and the "you" that refers to the relative or relatives in America seems to be less noticeable, so that we acquire the feeling that we are reading a journal kept with fair regularity. "His plan in regard to it," says Pierre Irving, "was to minute down notes in pencil in a small book, and extend them whenever he could seize a moment of leisure." With this material, supplemented by the family letters, the official biographer devoted to the first European journey of his distinguished uncle seven chapters of the memoirs, which occupied nearly a hundred pages and covered the entire period of travel, from July, 1804, to March, 1806. As we have seen, Pierre Irving made no very copious drafts upon the Journal, a fact for which we are not ungrateful, since sometimes the materials he preferred to use afford us useful supplementary information.

The traveller found himself so comfortably situated in Bordeaux that he did not set out for Toulouse until August 5th. The home of the ex-Mayor, M. Ferrier, in which he boarded, gave him good opportunities to improve his French and to gather some of the particulars with regard to Bordeaux, past and present, which he communicated to his American relatives. Perhaps it was from this source that he learned that the city was not nearly so populous as it was reputed to be, containing as it did only between eighty and ninety thousand souls. Two years before an English traveller had added sixty thousand to these figures. Whatever the size of the city, however, the number of American ships crowding the port for the sake of the wine trade was something that impressed all strangers, and gave great patriotic delight to the visitor in whom we are most concerned. His patriotism did not lead him to mention the rattlesnake kept in spirits in the museum, to which Miss Anne Plumptre, novelist, translator, and voyager, devoted a word, but he had a keen eye for most things of interest, from romantic ruins seen by moonlight to the queerly dressed fruit women, "bawling out their merchandize in a voice every tone of which is as sharp as vinegar." He is sufficiently inquisitive to ask questions with regard to the damages wrought by a storm of forty years before, and although he hopes, with the century of his birth, to become a "citizen of the world," although he quotes the famous passage from Congreve's *Mourning Bride* so much lauded by Dr. Johnson, although he indulges in proper reflections on the destruction caused during the French Revolution by the "unhallowed hands of tasteless barbarians," although he writes us, in a fashion becoming to a juvenile essayist, a little disquisition on the character of a sailor, we perceive that he is very far from being a stilted young prig. He enjoys meeting American girls, who please him much more than too "transparent and uncovered" French belles, he makes friends easily, he describes little incidents vividly — for example, the way the "pretty black eyed" shopwoman made the American sea-captain buy "a large hand organ for 400 livres (a third more than it was worth) which he did not know what the devil to do with after he had got it." Surely a most attractive young fellow, whom Providence did well to save from drowning, when, in his eagerness to get letters from a newly arrived vessel, he hired a boat to take himself and a friend on board, and in the dark night and dangerous current got entangled with a ship's cable. This touch of danger reminds us of the fact that the Europe Irving first visited was the Europe of Napoleon and of War. At Bordeaux, however, he saw no great signs of disturbance, and, although the Journal is not without its references to spies, soldiers, privateers, and passport difficulties, it is on the whole the record of an undisturbed and agreeable series of experiences.

The journey to Toulouse was made in a diligence, and we may well believe Irving when he says he was "highly delighted" with his trip. If he had not been, he neither would nor could have given so pleasant an account of it. Later we shall find him describing other expeditions by coach, and whatever his discomforts, he is always interesting in what he reports about his fellow passengers. His descriptions may not entitle him to a place among the masters of his craft in this category,— with Fielding, Balzac, De Quincey, Daudet, for example, — but surely the pages in which he tells us about his new found friend, Dr. Henry, the little, eccentric, bustling, bluffing American adventurer, are worth reading and remembering. It is true that Pierre Irving has already presented this original to us,— taking care, by the way, to improve his uncle's spelling and punctuation,— but it is to the early pages of the Journal that we must go if we wish to make the amusing little person's acquaintance as completely as is possible now that his genial ebullience has been extinguished these many years.

There is no need to dwell on the description of the journey taken from Toulouse "on board of a post boat of the canal of Languedoc," or, indeed, to follow our traveller closely through Southern France. Evidently he has a good eye for beauty of scenery, particularly of a pastoral kind, and he will later give us many pages of description worthy of a more practised pen. At Montpellier we learn that he has a temper, and that he will not allow himself to be imposed upon by rascally porters — furthermore, that one of the first things he does in a new place is to sample the theatre and to make intelligent remarks on the scenery and the acting. Fêtes, street crowds, pretty girls, also have their attractions for him, but they do not eclipse the amphitheatre at Nîmes, or the Maison Carrée of the same impressive city, or the superb prospect from the esplanade at Avignon. Long before John Stuart Mill sought this erstwhile capital of the Popes, Irving had written, doubtless thinking of his own precarious health, "It appears to me that Avignon would prove a most favorable residence for the valitudinarian in regard to beauty of Landscape and pleasant walks [,] tho I am unacquainted to what degree the climate is beneficial in this particular spot." Much, however, as he is fascinated by Nîmes and Avignon, he has not a word of regret for the fact that, in going from the former city to the latter and thence to Marseilles, he had no opportunity to see the unparalleled Pont du Gard or to examine the noble antiquities of Arles. He must have known of them, one fancies, for he was in the habit of reading rather carefully the observations of other travellers, on some of whom the splendor and the interest of the sights he missed had not been lost. Possibly he was more worried over the deficiencies of his passport than he liked to admit — with reason, as it will appear — possibly he made attempts to change his route, of which he has not informed us; possibly his reading of travel literature was done mainly in connection with Italy. Even to-day it is news to many educated people that Southern France vies with Italy itself in the matter of Roman antiquities. However all this may be, we find him arriving at Marseilles on the evening of August 21st after an unsatisfactory glimpse of the interesting town of Aix.

The varied population of the great seaport was very attractive to the young American, who could not help regretting that so few of his own country's ships were to be seen in the harbor. He soon learned that this was on account of the burdensome restrictions placed on commerce, Leghorn in consequence securing trade that would otherwise have come to the beautiful French port. A new acquaintance, Mr. Appleton of Boston, his ubiquitous friend, Dr. Henry, a city fair, a farcical balloon ascension, the theatre, an extraordinary specimen of the native Frenchman employed as consul by the far off and not yet opulent United States, these persons and sights occupied his time until September 10th, when he set out with Dr. Henry for Nice. Thus far it had been no "Sentimental Journey" — though we find him quoting Sterne — and it was to be even less so now, for although he ran no risk of running into a raging battle, it was still wartime and spies were abroad. He was suspected of being an Englishman, something was the matter with his passport, and to his great disgust he was held up at Nice for five long weeks. No wonder he feels "depressed by lonesomeness & chagrin." The charms of the scenery cannot make up for the anxiety and inconvenience caused by the delays of the post, or for the vexations due to the stupidity of suspicious officials. And even Dr. Henry now has to abandon him—apparently forever. Two or three consuls, the American Minister at Paris, Mr. Robert L. Livingston, and his own friend, Hall Storm, at Genoa come to his rescue, however, as speedily as they can, and time and youth heal much deeper wounds. On October 17th he "sat sail" in a felucca for Genoa.

His adventures along the coast need not detain us, nor need we give to his sojourn in Genoa an attention at all proportionate to its length. Although he dutifully informs his relatives with regard to the principal churches of the city and the pictures they contain, and although he makes his usual quota of comments on the theatre, it is not long before we gather the reason that keeps him from pursuing his travels until two months have slipped by. The charming daughters of Mrs. Bird, "lady of the English consul," make the village of Sestri a pleasant goal for excursions; Lord and Lady Shaftesbury and their daughter, Lady Barbara, to whom he is introduced by his friend Storm, are very cordial and prove to be attractive hosts, despite the eccentricities of the Earl — the fifth of his line — who has never got over the effects of a fall; private theatricals and dances, at which the surreptitious lessons of boyhood are put to good use, are naturally more alluring to a youth than lonely journeyings for the purpose of seeing sights that make for edification. As we shall see later, the brother who was furnishing the money for the tour had a right to chide Washington's fondness for company, which kept him overlong at Genoa and caused him to miss Florence and Venice entirely; but now that the youthful laughter of those gay companions has been stilled for more than a century, we can surely afford to be sparing of our own censures. Even if what he writes about churches and pictures is a bit perfunctory, he atones by writing with zest about Madame Brignoli's "Dillitanti theatre," about the charming peasant girl Angelina and her betrothed, and about the execution of the brigand Joseph Muzzo, "The Great Devil of Genoa." Having enjoyed all this, we are contented to let him go on his way after he has devoted a single paragraph to the fine pictures he has seen and has made one of his sparse references to Napoleon, news of whose coronation has just been received. Whether we shall accept his excuse for taking ship for Messina and not travelling through Italy is a matter of small consequence. It is more to the purpose to remark that without any self-consciousness he gives us evidence that his Genoese friends were as loth to have him go as he was to exchange their hospitality for the primitive entertainment he was likely to find in Sicily.

Irving set sail from Genoa, for the visit to Sicily that had been urged by his brother William, on December 23, 1804, on board the ship "Matilda," formerly a Charleston packet. At her very next going to sea, as we learn from the *Life and Letters*, she was wrecked, and her genial captain, Strong, of whom we get such pleasant glimpses in the Journal, was lost with her. The details of the voyage are unimportant with one dramatic exception, save in so far as Irving's descriptions, which, although not without touches of rhetoric, have much of the fresh charm of youth and genuineness, foreshadow the accomplished literary man who was destined to delight two continents. The dramatic exception just mentioned is the exciting experience of the "Matilda" with a privateer that fell little short of being a pirate. This incident, in which Irving behaved well, is so fully covered in the *Life and Letters* that we cannot assert that the present publication adds anything of importance to our knowledge of the matter. To read the account given in the Journal is, however, to obtain a vivid picture of the discomforts and dangers of travel during the Napoleonic period, and one little point should not remain unnoticed. The privateer threatened to carry the "Matilda" to Malta, and in searching Irving's papers the rascals found a letter of introduction to the governor of that island, whom Irving in his Journal calls "Sir —— Ball," and in a letter given in the *Life and Letters*, Sir Isaac Ball. He meant Sir Alexander John Ball, the distinguished naval officer, and if he had had a chance to present his letter—either through the privateer's bad offices, or through capture by a

British war vessel, for Genoa, without the "Matilda's" knowledge, had been declared blockaded! or through ability to accept the offer of passage to Malta made by the captain of a schooner at Messina— the future author of *The Sketch Book* would in all probability have come into official, if not friendly, personal contact with the writer of *The Ancient Mariner*. For Coleridge had reached Malta in April, 1804, had become the governor's secretary, and did not leave the island until September, 1805. The might-have-beens of literary biography are not of transcendent importance, but somehow one wishes one could connect two such men as Irving and Coleridge a little more closely than one can on the bare statement in the *Life and Letters* that Coleridge regarded the *Chronicle of Granada* as "the *chef d'œuvre* of its kind."

The first of January, 1805, found Irving lonely and picturing to himself "the cheerfulness, the good humor & hospitality that prevails through all ranks" in New York. But he enjoys the beautiful scenery and the delightful weather along the Italian coast, he both reads up on the regions he passes and retails classical commonplaces, and at last on the fifth of the month he enters the harbor of Messina, which, of all the cities he has seen, is in his opinion "the most charming to approach." Soon he had a good laugh at the shrinking of the health officer from hearty Captain Strong, who, it was feared, might be importing the germs of some pestilential disease. There was less laughing at the rigid quarantine to which all on board the "Matilda" were subjected. Our cooped-up youngster obtains details, however, about the American expedition to Tripoli, translates into English Italian books dealing with Sicily, makes acquaintance with American naval men, gets into scrapes with the local health officers, and manages to live through the twenty-one days of confinement. With them over we ourselves arrive at the last page of the first volume of the Journal.

The second volume begins at Messina under date of January 24, 1805. We may pass over Irving's stay at that city, still damaged by the famous earthquake of 1783, and may follow him to Syracuse, pausing only to refer to the slight but excellent picture he gives of Nelson's fleet. This is quoted in the *Life and Letters* with the remark that "In less than a year, Nelson's young admirer, who chronicled this animating spectacle, was one of thronging thousands that pressed to behold his remains as they lay in state at Greenwich, wrapped in the flag that now floated so proudly above him."

The great sailor was quickly out of Irving's ken,

but lesser naval figures were all around him, and with them he soon established very pleasant relations. Four American frigates and a brig of the force sent against Tripoli were at Syracuse, and the money they had circulated there had "given comparatively an air of life to the place." With friendly officers the young man went to theatre and ball and visited famous sights such as the "Ear of Dionysius," the secret chamber of which a former traveller—Brydone—had described as "totally inaccessible," but which the Americans managed to explore with some thoroughness. Then as now our countrymen were "enterprising," and in their encounters with the hectoring beggars of Syracuse they came off well. One of these Americans, however, was already longing for home. Irving was still enough of his sunny, genial self to get "a vast deal of amusement among the officers" at a masquerade by mingling with them in the character of an old physician, talking to them in broken English mixed with French and Italian, telling them anecdotes about themselves, and completely mystifying them until in an unguarded moment he happened not to disguise his voice. A day later, although he could write of leaving "Syracuse with extreme regret," he had hardly described the cavalcade of which he was a member—eleven men well armed against bandits—before he wrote: "I shall ever remember the delight I felt upon turning my back upon Syracuse. I had now reached the extremity of my tour; it seemed as if my face was turned homewards and that every step brought me nearer to America."

It is not literally true that with every step homeward he lost interest in his Journal, for some readable pages follow giving an account of his movements by land up to Catania, whence he proceeded across to Palermo, under conditions even then to be regarded as very primitive. But at Catania, where he spent some days and had his pocket picked in a "*sanctum sanctorum*," we come to a gap in the Journal that has to be made up with help of the pencilled Notes, the instalments devoted to Naples and Rome are not without their *longueurs*, there is again a break in the record—not, apparently, through Irving's fault—and the final instalment that takes him and us from Zurich through Paris and the Low Countries to England is scarcely comparable in zest and interest with the pages that describe his progress from Bordeaux to Syracuse, or even with those in the Notes that deal with Catania and the journey to Palermo. Outside of Sicily there are no visits to convents, where nuns ask for loaf sugar and seeds of American flowers— Irving and his friends had forgot to bring any! — there are no glimpses of a "Shepherd boy on the side of a hill near the valley of Enna playing on a reed," there is not so much opportunity to flog muleteers — the gentle Irving did not do the flogging — and, last but not least, there are no such informal invitations to take part in a masquerade as our young travellers received at Termini, where Irving had the honor of dancing with the daughter of his host, Baron Palmeria. Of this last adventure, as well as of a curious experience of the servant Louis, we have a better account in the *Life and Letters* given years later by Irving to his nephew, but we are glad to be able to read the original Notes, regretting the while that the remainder of the journey will cover better known regions and introduce us to much more sophisticated society.

It was Carnival time at Palermo, and our Americans were "completely peppered" with "sugar plumbs." In a hired "chariot" they joined the noble and well-to-do classes in the show on the promenade; they went to the theatre, where Irving had to be told to remove his hat while the Viceroy was in the house; they attended a dancing party; at the risk of not being deemed respectable, they saw the town on foot; and then, on the last day of February, 1805, they learned once more that friends must part. Irving went on board a small vessel bound for Naples, but the weather conditions were not sufficiently favorable until March 5th, when the final start was made. On the seventh, after enjoying "a full view" of the Bay of Naples, he landed safely and to his delight he found so many letters awaiting him that they crammed his pockets "like a post boys knapsack."

After keeping indoors writing letters, dining with bankers, meeting pleasant people, including an old German musician, who brought him copies of variations on "Yankee Doodle" and "Hail Columbia" — the Journal adds the touch that the recipient played the flute — Irving made in his Notes the following entry under date of March 11th:

"At eleven Oclock M[r] Degen calld on me & introduced me to a M[r] Cabel of Virginia and Col. Mercer one of the Commissioners of claims sent out to France. They arrived the day before yesterday from Rome. I was highly pleased with Cabel whom I had heard particular mention of before."

It was the first of these two Virginians, Joseph C. Cabell, afterwards closely associated with Jefferson in the founding of the University of Virginia, who was mainly responsible for William Irving's chagrin at the number of things Washington Irving did not see on his first visit to Italy. Cabell was a delightful companion who was much pleased with Irving, and the two young men naturally wished to keep together. The Virginian, however, had already seen some of the things the New Yorker's brother wanted his own ward to see. Those not being the days of cablegrams, we are not surprised to find the note immediately succeeding the one already quoted beginning as follows: "24th [March] Sat off for Rome in com^{y} with Mr Cabell."

The interval between the 12th and the 24th was filled with rides to places of interest, with dinners, "conversaziones," and other social pleasures, and the Journal for the earlier days was very faithfully, yet not too perfunctorily, written out. Perhaps Irving used for this purpose some of the leisure that came to him in consequence of the violent cold in his face which confined him to his room for three days. He was not so ill that he could not enjoy watching and describing the sights outside his window, particularly the sulky-accident that befell a dissolute young English nobleman belonging to the Navy, who had "come to Naples with the spirited determination of *astonishing* the natives a few." By the 22d, the temporary invalid could join Cabell—Colonel Mercer had sailed for Marseilles—in a carriage ride to the Grotto del Cane; on the 24th, as we have seen, they left Naples; on the afternoon of the 27th they entered Rome by the Lateran Gate. The Journal continues to be exemplarily full, but some readers may find it a bit too hackneyed and literary, and this may be felt to be especially true of the portion dealing with the short stay in Rome. It must be remembered in Irving's defence that, after he left Sicily, he more or less trod familiar ground, that he was writing, not for the public—certainly not for the public of more than a century later—but for relatives eager to enjoy every word he could send them—and that, all things considered, his descriptions are good, his comments sound if sometimes trite, and the information he imparts solid, and, as his generation would have said, "improving." We infer that he sometimes met improving people, as when he mentions that he was accosted at the Museum of Herculaneum by an English antiquarian of his acquaintance, the Rev. Mr. Heyter. The learned gentleman is easily identified as the Rev. John Hayter, who had still thirteen years to live, and has his niche in the great *Dictionary of National Biography*.

An acquaintance more important to Irving was made in Rome, the poet-painter Washington Allston. With such friends as Allston and Cabell, and with so much to see in a little over two weeks, the young man can have had but slight time for reflection or for homesickness. The sights he saw—most of them what every one now sees that makes even a superficial tour of Europe—need not detain us, but we should not forget to observe the references to Canova, to Baron Humboldt, the Prussian Minister, who was a little later of service to Coleridge, and, brief though it be, to Madame de Staël, whose *Corinne* had not yet appeared. We may note also the honest confession that the diarist was "satiated with antique statues," and the fact that sometimes his pages almost degenerate into a catalogue. Perhaps it was just as well that he did not attempt to realize his passing dream of staying in Rome with Allston and becoming a painter. He was probably better qualified to quote poetry—*Childe Harold* was not yet ready to his hand, nor was Keats yet buried near the pyramid of Caius Sestius—and, on occasion, to deal firmly with extortionate rascals, as on the excursion to Frascati.

After witnessing the ceremonies of Holy Week, less important than usual on account of the absence of Pope Pius VII, Irving and Cabell left Rome for Bologna, accompanied by a faithful servant, a native of Brussels, John Josse Vandermoere. One of Irving's reasons for haste, as we learn from a letter to William, was the desire for Cabell's company and for the latter's assistance in Paris, where he was well acquainted. Paris Irving was eager to reach that he might rest from his wanderings and "pay attention to several branches of art and science into which" he wished "to get a little insight." Another letter mentions as an inducement a course of lectures due to commence in May "at the Garden of Plants in Paris." We need not dwell on these excuses, but may note with his biographer that what we know of Irving's first visit to Paris indicates a far more assiduous attendance upon theatres than upon lectures on botany, although he did not entirely neglect the latter. Nice, natural boy! Should we like him half so well if he had not made respectably plausible excuses for his conduct, and had not gone to the theatre whenever he could? But we must sympathize also with the chiding brother who wrote, "your skipping through Italy, omitting to visit Florence and Venice, I cannot forget."

The second volume of the Journal breaks off in Rome on April 13th, 1805, and the fourth volume begins on May 17th, the day after the travellers drove out of Zurich. The missing third volume must therefore have covered the journey to and the stay in the latter city. For the portion of the tour thus unrecorded in full we have a few pages of Notes describing the trip from Rome to Ancona, reached on April 19th, and a larger instalment of the same jottings covering the route from Lake Maggiore, where Sesto was left on May 3rd, to Altorf, where the young friends, who liked the simple Swiss folk, parted with their honest landlord and his wife on the cold morning of May 10th. The *Life and Letters* prove, even if Irving's own enumeration "Vol. 4th" were not sufficient, that there was a third volume of the Journal, but the biographer gives us only a slight extract from it relating to Bologna, outlines the route to Milan by way of Modena, Parma, Piacenza, and Lodi, and adds a few details about Milan, where the tourists arrived on April 29th, greatly fatigued. They had seen so much in such a short time that it is unlikely that, when the third volume of the Journal emerges from its hiding-place, it will be found to contain much of interest apart from the purely personal touches. Meanwhile we may be glad that the Notes give Irving's share of the expenses of the trip, reckoned at Bologna on April 23rd. His memoranda require no farther comment, perhaps, except a reference to the broadness of the conversation carried on with the landlady and her daughters at "the very miserable village of Iornina." It is the taste of the eighteenth century that characterizes our travellers, not that of the twentieth.

The twentieth century, however, eschews long introductions almost as strenuously as it does broad conversations, more strenuously than it does when the latter are reported, as in the Notes, in that delicate and complaisant language, the French. Fortunately this introduction can now hurry rapidly to its end, for not only is the fourth volume of the Journal short, but it is also comparatively unimportant, omitting as it does Irving's stay in Paris from May 24th to September 22nd, 1805. Both in getting us to and in taking us from the great and beautiful capital Irving shows that he has not forgotten how to describe in an interesting fashion his fellow occupants of a stagecoach. He is pleased when they display an intelligent curiosity about America, which he expects from her peaceful situation to take the first place among the nations. He does not conceal his indignation at the governments that spread false stories about the New World in order to discourage emigration, but he has no word to say about those of his own countrymen who deluded poor people into coming to a land that was far from being the paradise the crafty agents had described. As we all have done and still do, he notes with amusement the extraordinary ignorance about America to be found on every hand. He gives us also an entertaining glimpse of Mr. Cabell's efforts to make love to a girl in the diligence, he sketches well an importunate barber and an irate landlady — the latter perhaps not so much at fault as he would have us think, for young men are thoughtless, and sometimes provincial folk do not understand an American traveller's French — he lets us know he has no use for lap-dogs, he reports a eulogy of Moreau, the victor of Hohenlinden and the rival of Bonaparte. One wishes that he had found time at least to describe some of the acting he saw in Paris and to tell us about the farewell dinner he seems to have given his friends in the gay city; but one must content one's self with beginning another journey with him by coach in company with Mr. Massie of Virginia and Mr. Gorham of Boston.

The encounter at Valenciennes — not a military one, though the strength of the fortifications is duly noted — with Mr. Charles Heems, "a strangely impertinent fellow," who pretended to know many distinguished Americans, but could scarcely understand a word of English, is a clear indication that this portion of the Journal, though dwindling in importance, still retains interest. The description of Brussels is perhaps all that can be expected of a traveller who makes so short a stay, and this may be said about the remarks upon what little of Holland the young man saw. He spoke no Dutch, and it is evident that he had no great sympathy with the land and its people—a fact which may make this portion of the Journal useful to some future critic of *Knickerbocker's History of New York.* On October 4th, he sets sail for the country which, after America, is to share his heart with Spain, and curiously enough he sails from Rotterdam to England in a boat flying Prussian colors under the connivance of a French official! War has its exigencies, and time brings changes. Early in the following morning he gets his first glimpses "of Old England," and he finds that English villages please him more than those of France and Italy.

He was soon, however, to be in a position to declare that in respect to the stupidity of their officials the three countries were about on a par. There was delay at Gravesend over his passport, and it was not until the ninth that he could go on shore. There a letter from the American Minister, the future President Monroe, explained some at least of the causes of the trouble. With a Prussian traveller, also detained, the young man hired a post-chaise and was soon in London, where, though "surrounded by haughty English," he determined "to excel their pride by tenfold," gathered his forces for attack, "and was perhaps the proudest spirited fellow in London the whole afternoon." Nevertheless, he feels that in England he is a man, while in affable France he was "a cypher — a worm that might have been crushed with impunity." Fundamentally he is a Briton, and a fortunate boy as well, for after having had his "taste changed and vitiated by France," he sees Mrs. Siddons and is "at peace" with himself. How little the world alters with the centuries, and how easily in matters connected with country or race we become unconscious hypocrites, not to say smug imbeciles! How easily also do we recognize in the charming fellow we have landed safely in the England he is later to describe with such fidelity and devotion the prototype in many respects of the young Americans who engage our affections in the present year of grace. The old order changes, but not without bequeathing to the new a heritage more valuable than the heir is usually willing at first to acknowledge.

W. P. Trent.

NOTE

The Grolier Club expresses its appreciative thanks to Mrs. Isaac N. Seligman and Mr. William A. White for their kind permission to publish these Journals from the original manuscripts belonging to them respectively. The first of the three vellum-bound blank books comprising the Journals consists of one hundred and fifteen closely written leaves of blue paper, with rough pencil drawings on the insides of the covers and on a fly-leaf, and notes, such as "Ship Matilda 27th Decr Opposite Corsica" and "Acheté en Bordeaux Juillet 1804 *Prix* 3 *liv." The "Second" and "Fourth" volumes are similar, but slightly smaller, and not so thick. The much smaller volume of preliminary notes, which has been used to cover the comparatively short period for which there seems to have been a missing third volume of the elaborated Journal, was generously lent to the Club by the late Mr. Irving Van Wart. It is one of a series, and became, after his death, a part of Mrs. Seligman's collection.*

The transcripts for the printer have been diligently compared with the original manuscripts by Miss Ruth S. Granniss, Librarian of the Club, who has supplied the Notes on the Text. The work of comparison was carried on in the Manuscript Division of the New York Public Library, and the courtesy and assistance received there are gratefully acknowledged. In transcribing the manuscripts, Irving's spelling and punctuation have been followed, except in cases where it has seemed advisable to carry out his obvious intention, as in the supplying of periods where he occasionally indicated the beginning of new sentences merely by extra spacing, etc. Proper nouns and adjectives have been capitalized where necessary, but attention has not been drawn to the frequent misspelling of names, except where it has seemed necessary to avoid confusion.

In appearance, these volumes are purposed to suggest the books issued during the first quarter of the nineteenth century.

JOURNAL

OF A

TOUR THRO FRANCE, ITALY

SICILY

NOTES & JOURNAL
OF
TRAVEL IN EUROPE

Bordeaux, July 1st 1804

My dear Brother

YESTERDAY morning for the first time I set foot on European land, in this city, after having been forty two days on Ship board (we set sail from New York the 19th May). Our paſsage was mild and pleasant, and what the sailors term "a lady's Voyage." We were delay'd by head winds and calms, particularly after we entered the Bay of Biscay. In consequence of these head winds the first land we made was Cape Peñas on the coast of Spain. The land rose from the shore into vast mountains of rock that lifted their snowy heads far above the clouds. After standing on another tack and losing sight of land we were several days before we made Cordovan light house which we did on the 25 June and anchored the same afternoon in Verdun roads, mouth of the Gironne, where we were obliged to remain three days at quarantine in compliance with a rule observed towards all veſsels from America.

The Gironne is formed by the junction of the

Dordogne and the Garonne which takes place a few leagues below Bordeaux. The Garonne has its source in the Pyrenees and is the river on the banks of which Bordeaux is situated.

Our sail up the river was delightful. At first the river was wide and the land very low but altered as we proceeded and the latter part was charming. The country adjacent is sandy, but is famous for producing the Medoc & other wines that are counted the best in France.

The Hills and vales were covered with Vineyards of a rich & lively green to which the white walls of the Villages and chatteaux afforded a pleasing contrast. Frequently on the Banks of the river were seen cottages embowered in groves of elm's and their white washed walls over run with Vines. They reminded me of those delightful retreats of rural happineſs so often sung by our pastoral poets and had but the muddy Garonne have *roll'd a silver wave* I should have pronounced the picture complete.

On our arrival we had to parade about the city in a body to the Admiralty & municipality offices to have our protections &c examined signd seald &c. As there were seventeen paſsengers of us, all French except myself and several of them pretty looking personages enough you may imagine we made a tolterably amusing proceſsion. These things are not however noticed in France, where they are used to ridiculous sights & manouvres.

July 7th

I have now been a week in Bordeaux and my ideas begin to collect again, for I afsure you they have been quite in a state of derangement since my arrival, from the Novelty of my situation.

The letters of introduction I brought for this city have procured me the most hospitable attentions. I am in the family of a Mons Ferrier, an old Gentleman who some time since was one of the richest and most respectable Merchants in this place and for some time Mayor of the City, but a succefsion of misfortunes have stripped him of most of his property. He has still enough however, to support him in an easy genteel style, his house is handsomely furnished and his table both plentiful and elegant. He has also an estate in the country. The family consists of the old gentleman the old lady & myself besides three servants. They are a most amiable old couple, highly estimated and visited by the most respectable people in Bordeaux. They do not speak English, and their French is free from the barberous Gascon accent & dialect that prevails in this part of France so that I have an excellent opportunity to improve in the language. I am admitted in this family as a favor at the particular reccommendation of Dr Ellison formerly of New York now resident here, and I am universally congratulated on my good fortune

I am gradually becoming accustomed to the looks of Bordeaux. Its narrow streets and high stone buildings no longer appear singular. There is a strength and solidity about the houses that gives them an air of dignity we do not find in our light American buildings. They are built entirely of a kind of lime stone procured from quarries a few miles down the Garonne. This stone has some qualities that render it very excellent for building — when fresh from the Quarry it is soft and easily cut & shaped, and acquires by age & exposure to the air a considerable degree of hardneſs. At the same time however it loses that beautiful whiteneſs that distinguishes it at first and becomes in time black and dirty. This injures the looks of their edifices, as they do not think of painting or white washing them on the outside.

The rooms are high, & generally with floors of stone marble or tyle which gives them a delightful coolneſs in summer, and I am told they are very warm in winter when the floors are covered with carpets. The fronts of their houses are decorated with sculpture and iron raild balconies to the casements.

Among the chief antiquities of this place is the Palais Galien. It is the remains of a Roman Ampitheatre built under the reign of the Emperor Galien towards the middle of the third century. It is constructed of the same kind of stone with which Bordeaux is built, intermingled with brick.

Since the revolution the land on which it stands was sold in common with other National property and the purchasers began demolishing the building to make way for streets and houses. Fortunately however a Gentleman of taste arrived from Paris in quality of Préfet of this Department and rescued the precious remain of antiquity from entire demolition. The municipality have received a charge to look to its preservation so that there are hopes of its still existing a considerable time. Nothing however stands but part of the bare walls and one of the grand entrances, and it is merely the antiquity that entitles it to notice. This ampitheatre has not served as a place of amusement to the Romans alone. In poring over an old book entitled "Cronique Bourdelaise" I find that about two centurys ago some *bon vivants* of the infernal regions used to meet there to amuse themselves. An unfortunate chap who I suppose happened to be too knowing for the common run of folks was accused of sorcery, condemnd & executed. Before his death he confefsed having been at a meeting of some of these merry devils in the Palais Galien. I regard this ancient pile with peculiar reverence. It stands near my lodgings so that I frequently paſs it, and two or three times I have strolld home at night thro its silent ruins, and as I paſsd under the dark arches of the grand entrance I have almost expected to see an old Roman stalking amid the gloom.

The Grand Theatre is a magnificent building and said to be the finest of its kind in Europe. The outside is superb but the interior did not answer my expectations. By the interior I mean the audience part, for the grand enterance staircase &c is superb. The painting of the audience part is much soild and faded which considerably injures its appearance We complain very much in New York of our theatres being badly lighted; in Bordeaux they are far worse, having no light but what is given by a chandelier hung up in the centre. The stage also is not so well lighted as ours.

I have been twice to see La Fond one of the two first tragedians in France. He is performing here for a few nights after which he returns to Paris. Tho' I could not understand the language yet I was highly pleased with the Actor. His figure is tall and well made, his face uncommonly expreſsive—and his voice full and sonorous. The other actors were very indifferent, their gesticulations were violent and their attitudes often straind and unnatural. The Scenery is well executed the drefses rich with great attention to *costume.*

There are two or three other theatres of inferior merits, one of them called the théâtre Française is nearly as large as our theatre, but the actors are miserable. These lower order of theatres are great resorts for women of bad character, and are complete hot beds of vice & infamy. In front of one of the meanest a Jack pudding was mounted on a stage endeavoring to attract the multitude by his tricks and jokes.

July 9th

The people of Bordeaux exercise a liberty of speech that at first surprized me. They make no scruple of talking very freely among themselves concerning the Emperor and his conduct. This I am told is not noticed by the police as long as it is done in private, but should they exprefs their sentiments publicly and endeavor to instill them in the minds of others, they would certainly involve themselves in trouble.

In New York you have an idea that France is in a state of agitation and confusion in consequence of the war and the preparations for the invasion. As yet I have seen nothing of the kind. Every thing apparantly goes on with smoothnefs and regularity. No armed forces are seen parading the Streets. No drums or cannons to be heard. All is order and tranquility and did I not know to the contrary I should think them in peace with all the world.

The Merchants appear to be the chief sufferers as I see their Vefsels laid up in the river totally dismantled of their rigging, and they universally complain of want of businefs. The American Vefsels crowd the port and enjoy a fine harvest during the contests of Europe. It is only from seeing soldiers posted at the public places that I reccollect I am under a government in a certain degree military. A Stranger while he conducts himself with propriety may walk the streets continually & frequent every place of curiosity businefs or amusement apparantly unnoticed and unknown, but let him once behave in an improper or suspicious manner and he will find his every movement is observed. To this strictnefs of the police may be ascribed in a great degree the personal security & public tranquility in France.

The roads & highways throughout the country are patrolled by troops of Gens d'armes who visit the different taverns & houses and acquaint themselves with the manner of living and mode of subsistence of the inhabitants. The cities swarm with spies in every direction. In consequence, the streets & lanes may be traversed & the roads and high ways travelled at any time night or day without any danger of depredation or insult. Were this not the case every thing might be apprehended from the number of poor people and beggars with which this country abounds.

July 10th

It amuses me very much to walk the streets and observe the many ways these people have of getting a living of which we have no idea in America. The fruit women divert me the most, to see them with old fashioned long wasted drefses their arms stuck akimbo, monstrous caps on their heads the whole surmounted with a huge basket of fruit, thus decked off they straddle along the pavement bawling out their merchandize in a voice every tone of which is as sharp as vinegar. Beside these we have pedlars, shoe blacks, tumblers & Savoyards with their musical instruments, at every corner. And now and then we have a grand concert vocal & instrumental from half a dozen Italian peasant women with fiddles & tamborines.

The streets are entirely free from the broils & boxing matches one would expect in such a medley. A drunken man is rarely seen & generally proves to be some American who has been *enjoying* himself. Our countrymen have got a name for drunkenefs among this temperate people, and often when there is any disturbance at a public place of amusement it is common for the French to say— "pho—its only some drunken American or other." This vice which they consider unpardonable among themselves, they excuse in an American, they say "it is the custom of his country."

My situation in the family of Mr F is so agreeable that I think of lengthening my stay in this place, beyond what I first intended. I shall then be enabled to travel with more pleasure & advantage from having a better acquaintance with the language. I shall escape considerable of the hot weather that prevails at this season in the south of France and what is best of all, about the time I commence my journey the vintage will have began and I shall see the country and inhabitants in their happiest moments—all mirth and festivity.

The weather when I first arrived was uncommonly hot for this climate. Some of the old inhabitants afsure me they have never before experienced such heat in Bordeaux, it has since moderated exceedingly. The heat here is not so opprefsive and enervating as in New York and the evenings are cool & delightful. There are some very pleasant walks in this city one of which was formerly a vast garden open to the better order of people; since the revolution it has become common to all ranks & is called the Champ de Mars. It no longer contains beds of flowrs &c but there are several fine alleys & groves of trees which render it a delightful promenade. There is also a beautiful walk in the centre of one of the public streets called the Rue Tourney—it has three rows of fine elms with stone benches under them and is a very fashionable place of resort in the evening.

Amid all the scenes of novelty & pleasure that surround me, I afsure you my thoughts often return to New York with the most lively emotions. The idea that I am alone, far from my friends without opportunities of frequent communication "a stranger and a sojourner in the land" often throws a damp over my spirits which I find it difficult to shake off. This however I hope will wear away in time as I become more a "citizen of the World." Accustomed to be surrounded by those who took a near interest in my welfare it is a painful thought to indulge, that I am now left to my own self; to work my way among strangers who are indifferent to me and my concerns excepting as far as they can further their own interests.

July 12th

Yesterday afternoon I spent most agreeably in viewing one of the finest specimens of Gothic Architecture in France. This was the Cathederal church of St André. It was built by the English when in posſesſion of this city in the eleventh or twelvth century. The style of architecture is said to be extremely similar to that of Westminster Abbey in London and bears about it an air of indiscribable dignity and solemnity. The first view of it brought strongly to my reccollection the words of Congreve

How reverend is the face of this tall pile
Whose ancient pillars rear their marble heads
To bear aloft its arched & pondrous roof
By its own weight made steadfast & immovable
Looking tranquility it strikes an awe

It is a vast building, entirely of stone & decorated with all that profusion of carved work and minute ornament that characterizes the Gothic style. When inside, the lofty roof of arched work the vast pillars, the windows of painted glaſs had a *tout ensemble* that awakend awe & veneration The effects of the revolution are discernable in this building. The unhallowed hands of tasteless barbarians have stripped many of the paintings from the walls, have torn the images of the saints from the niches of which they had held quiet poſseſsion for centuries, and have decapitated several of the cardinals who mounted guard over the grand portal. Still however they could not injure materially, the beauty of the main Architecture, the undertaking would have required too much labor & time for the patience of a mob. The church has since been cleaned, is undergoing repairs in several places and has again become "the house of prayer." Our company consisted of five and we procured the sexton to shew us the way to the top of one of the grand towers, of which there are two. Our ascent was quite intricate and reminded me of some of those winding & perplexed paſsages thro which some of the heroes of modern romances wander when prowling about the interior of an old castle. In some places we had to ascend stone stair cases that wound up round towers of about six feet diameter & dimly lighted by narrow apertures in the wall. We then had to paſs thro narrow paſsages in the wall of the church having now and then on one side small square holes that looked into the interior of the building and on the other side similar ones that gave us a peep into the city. In one place our route entered the church and formed a narrow gallery almost as high as the ceiling or roof from whence we could see the people far below us at their prayers. In another place we had to walk on a kind of stone Cornice that ran round part of the outside of the edifice. After a great deal of this winding and twisting we at last arrived on the highest accefsible part of one of the steeples. The view from this place was vast and interesting. Beneath us lay the city presenting a singular *mêlange* of Architecture of different orders & periods. Beyond it the beautiful harbor in form of a crescent crowded with the ships of *my country*. And all around in the distance, a level country covered with Vineyards, diversified by chateaus and enlivened by the waters of the Garonne.

From the square part of the steeple on which we stood there rose a spire of about an hundred & twenty or thirty feet. It tapered to a point and we could stand in the inside and see to the very top of it as there were no stairs nor any wooden work in the interior. It is built entirely of stone with windows to the very top, and what surprized me was that the walls were not a foot in thicknefs, this gave it a dangerous appearance, particularly as I observed cracks in several places secured by bars of iron. There is another spire exactly similar to this in another part of the church, five or six feet of the top was struck off some time since, by lightening. After having remaind here for some time & witneſsed a beautiful sunset, we set out to retrace the labyrinth by which we ascended, and arrived safe on terra firma without any bruises or dislocations.

As this was the first gothic building I had seen it made particular impreſsion on my fancy and in fact it was some time before I could recall my eyes from hurrying over the whole & endeavoring to grasp a full view of every part to the more satisfactory manner of deliberate examination. No doubt I give a high colord description of some objects for every thing is heightend to me by Novelty

[*July*] 13th

The newspapers of France are extremely barren of intelligence and observe the greatest caution about mentioning the designs or actions of Government.

Indeed the movements of the executive are conducted with so much secrecy that they are rarely anticipated, nor do the editors of papers dare to indulge themselves in comments or animadversions. One paper in Paris the other day entitled the *Publiciste* inserted some conjectures respecting the intention of France toward Italy. The gazette was immediately stopped and it was with great difficulty it was permitted to go on again after two days ceſsation on condition of changing its editor. This affords a striking contrast to that liberty of the prefs that prevails in America, where every public measure or public character is attacked with indiscriminate inveteracy in the Newspapers. In consequence of this silence in the French papers we have but little political news stirring and it is only by vague rumors, we hear what is going on at the seat of Government. The Quid nuncs of New York hear far more about the concerns of France than her own citizens for those of whom I enquire seem to have nothing but surmises & uncertain reports to give me.

A great part of the polite world of Bordeaux have gone to take the waters of Bagnères, a small town among the Pyrenees famous for its mineral springs, & a fashionable place of resort from different parts of France. The air of that town is said to be cool & salubrious in the midst of summer and its situation among the mountains gives it the advantage of a vast variety of grand & romantic scenery. Probably it is owing to this fashionable desertion that I may attribute the great scarcity of beauty that prevails at Bordeaux, for I have hardly seen a lady since my arrival that I would call handsome. They have also a manner of drefsing their heads that I do not admire. They torture the hair into unnatural twists & ringlets and lard it over with a profusion of *ancient oil*. My objection to this mode may arise from its reminding me of the greasy locks of the squaws I have seen in Canada. At any rate, it cannot be equal in beauty in the eyes of an unprejudiced person, to light fanciful ringlets of hair dry & elastic, that play with every zephyr. The drefs of the French ladies is also unpleasing to me, tho' I was partly prepared for it by the light robes of our *transparent élégantes.*

July 14th

I have been this evening to visit a garden about three miles out of the city owned by an old gentleman of great property who has his country house there. He is unmarried and takes great pride in having his garden admired. It is open to the public at all times, free of expence. The garden is very extensive laid out in the old taste of clipd walks alleys arbors &c. It has a very pretty effect on the eye for the first time, but there is a degree of samenefs in the walks &c that soon grows tiresome. The old gentlemen has certainly been at a vast expence to please the public, and the least they can do in return is to admire his works. This garden is a great place of resort for the lower clafses on Sunday, as they can enjoy themselves there free of expence.

Sunday is still considered in France as a day of relaxation and amusement, and little of that attention to religious ceremonies that prevaild before the revolution, is observable at present. Tis true however that the churches are again opened and many go there to perform their devotions but they appear to hurry thro them with indifference that they may return to their busineſs, or pleasures. Many of the stores &c are open all Sunday, and the streets are throngd with itinerent merchants as on other days. The theatres, gardens & other places of amusement are crowded on Sunday evenings in short it is a perfect holiday. Such of the merchants & principal inhabitants as can afford it have a country house just out of the city, where they retire on Saturday evening with their families and enjoy the air of the country & dust of the roads till the next evening.

July 15th

This morning I went with three or four others to view the church of St Michel. After viewing St André's there is nothing in the architecture of this church capable of exciting admiration We ascended the steeple which stands at a little distance from the main body of the church, and enjoyed a very fine prospect from the top of it. The spire, which was of stone & very high, was blown down in a storm about thirty or forty years since, I could not learn if it did much damage in the neighborhood. In a vaulted appartment under this tower are several bodies of persons who have been dead a long time. They have been taken out of the family vaults of the church to make room for fresh corpses. The skeletons remain entire and are covered with the skin as dry as parchment. They were ranged about the wall without order & many had fallen to the ground and were troddn to pieces. The fellow who bore the light and shewed them to us, handled them & tofsed them about without ceremony. It reminded me strongly of the gravedigger scene in Hamlet. Here was a true picture of the equality to which Death reduces us. Persons of all ranks and descriptions crowded promiscuously together. In one corner the body of a belle leaned against that of a beggar, and in another a Chevalier of the order of St Louis was the intimate neighbor of a common Porter!

After leaving the church we visited the museum. This is an institution commenced since the revolution. The collection is small but very prettily arranged.

In the afternoon I went out of town to dine with Mr Jonathan Jones and his family at their country house. The afternoon pafsed delightfully. The old gentleman is extremely sociable & good humored, Mrs Jones is very agreeable, & he has two daughters the finest girls I have seen in Bordeaux. The girls talk English tolerably well, drefs in the American style considerably and resemble very much the young ladies of New York. Perhaps this latter circumstance reccommended them more to me than any other for I confefs I have not yet got rid of my prejudices in favor of the American girls.

[*July*] 17th

The French trades people display a very pretty taste in the arrangement & decorations of their shops &c. This is particularly observable in the shops of the Milliners, the confectioners and other dealers in fashions and delicacies. The principal streets have a gay look from this circumstance and a stranger is tempted at every turn, to purchase, from the pretty and inviting manner in which the merchandize is spread to view. The trades people also seem to be great adepts in the art of persuasion and with a very little knowledge of the English language and an infinite share of adroitness and insinuation, they can manage to make some of our simple countrymen purchase a thousand things they have no occasion for.

I was highly amused the other day with a specimen of their ingenuity in this particular. I went to the Exchange with an honest American captain and as the hour of change had not commenced we amused ourselves with walking in a wide lobby that runs round the change room, and on each side of which are arranged *Boutiques* or stalls of all kinds of merchandize, jewelry millinary literary &c &c ad infin. The Captain stopped before one of the Boutiques where a variety of musical instruments were offered for sale to price a very small hand organ, which he thought of purchasing to teach a bird to whistle.

The stall was kept by a pretty little black eyed woman who could make out to prattle a little bad English. She immediately had a dozen instruments spread before the Captain. He however did not want one for the present and we were turning to go away when she begged we would accompany [her] to a ware house she had close by where she would shew us some fine instruments. The Captain turnd to me & wispered with a knowing wink "Dam'me lets go and over haul her trumpery, youl see how she'll try to come along side of us, but the devil a sou do I lay out for her fiddles or music mills." We accordingly accompanied her, to her ware room in the second story of a neighboring house. Here she displayed a fine afsortment of organs & hurdy gurdys, played Hail Columbia, Yankee Doodle, got her husband to play on the forte piano, uncorked a bottle of wine & made us drink, in short, I cannot tell one tenth of her manouevres but by the help of Music & wine and flattery & a pretty face the honest Captain was so bewildered that before he got out of the ware room he had bought a large hand organ for 400 livres (a third more than it was worth) which he did not know what the devil to do with after he had got it.

[*July*] 25th

I was witneſs to a little ceremony the other day that pleased me more than many that I have seen of the kind that were accompanied with infinitely superior shew & grandeur. It was a funeral. An American Sailor had been drowned and several of his Brother Tars had aſsembled to pay the last tribute of respect to his memory. The coffin was carried on a Bier, preceded by the American flag spread horizontally and the corners held by four sailors. After the corps, the [*blank*] of the ship was carried in the same manner and was followed by the remainder of the ships crew. The deceased, I found out had been a great favorite among his meſsmates—a "fellow of infinite jest," much like Dibdin's "Tom Bowling." His loſs had been sensibly felt by them, and the ceremony I had just seen had been dictated by the honest affections of their hearts.

Tho I am not one of those who ascribe almost every virtue to the character of a sailor, yet I confefs there are often such genuine traits of honest worth displayed by this clafs of beings, that I do not wonder they gain more credit than they deserve. Removed from intimate intercourse with the world, placed among men carelefs and simple in manner as himself, the sailor does not acquire that habit of hypocricy & simulation common in society. He has no need to disguise his feelings or affect a different character than the one he pofsefses. Of course all his good deeds are spontaneous, his attachments sincere & uninterested. Conscious of no deceit in himself he suspects none in others and displays a franknefs and openefs of conduct extremely prepofsefsing. He sets no value on money except as it contributes to his pleasure and gratification and squanders or gives it way with a freedom that is often mistaken for generosity.

[*July*] 28th

The most fashionable evening promenade in Bordeaux is the Tourney. This is a walk shaded by three rows of trees in the centre of one of the principal streets. It presents an entertaining mélange of figures & characters. Whether it is, that I am accustomed to the strange looking beings in New York or not, I cannot say, but it appears to me there is a greater proportion of *outré* objects among the French, than with us. The females drefs in three distinct modes indicative of their situations & ranks, tho there are intermediate modes proportioned to the circumstances of the wearers. Of the Belles you may form some idea from our élégantes in New York tho' they are rather more transparent and uncovered here. The daughters of tradesmen & mechanics, drefs very neatly and have a trim appearance, they wear a high cap with a narrow border round the face that has a pretty effect. The Servant girls, fruit women &c wear long waists large caps with enormous borders that appear like wings on each side of their heads and at a little distance look like old women. As to the men there is an endlefs variety in their drefs and appearance. You may imagine therefore that a public walk crowded with such a diversity of objects must be amusing to a stranger. But besides these, there are jugglers musicians and mountebanks of one kind or another continually presenting themselves. I was walking the Tourney this evening when I was attracted to the piazza of a handsome coffee house by a number of Savoyards male & female who were playing on three or four kinds of instruments and singing, their music was very pretty and the airs simple & sweet. After they had finished a girl went round with a little plate to receive the donations of the audience that had collected. Walking a little farther I encountered another crowd who surrounded a Quack, whose [?] was decorated with stuffed mole skins, a curious sea fish &c and surmounted by a tame hawk—he had a rat in a cage which played many tricks at the word of command, after he had collected a sufficient crowd, he opened a box and began to sell his drugs descanting upon the merits of every one of them, and proving them all infallible.

A little further on, a Juggler was playing to another respectable circle, and performing tricks with eggs cards &c. His wife danced a hornpipe and two or three of his children tumbled. As soon as they had gone thro' their routine of tricks his wife collected a few sous from such of the crowd as appeared most able to give them and then the husband commenced opperating in another branch of his profefsion. This was as a fortune teller. None of his audience however seemed anxious to peep into futurity, when casting his eyes around he happened to catch a glimpse of me as I stood a little distant from the throng in company with a young Frenchman. The juggler immediately exclaimed, pointing at me, "voilà un homme de bonheur, venez ici Monsieur venez ici." As I had no inclination to have my destiny proclaimed to the world I decamped from his neighborhood as soon as pofsible.

It is impofsible to conceive the various modes the lower orders in Europe have of getting a livelihood, unknown in America. Nothing is thrown away here, and it is certain that a poor Frenchman can live on almost nothing.

Aug. 2d

AS I intend leaving this place tomorrow I have been all over the city this morning & afternoon to take a farewell look, and to see such objects of curiosity as I had hitherto neglected. In the course of my tour I was in several churches of lefs note than those I have before mentioned. Some of them are undergoing repairs in those parts that have been injured during the revolution. It is painful to see so many fine specimens of the arts that have been the pride of ages long since pafsed away, defaced by the blind fury of a misguided populace. In one place I saw the ruins of what had once been a handsome church. The steeple was still standing by itself and will probably one day or other bring down vengeance on the heads of its persecutors.

In the afternoon I visited the church and convent of the Chartreuse. The holy fathers have long since been obliged to evacuate this habitation which at present is converted into a hospital for negroes. This church however is still in a good state. It is small but very handsome. The Altar place is the most superb I have seen in Bordeaux. The walls of the church are painted in arches columns Galleries &c. The painting is well executed and makes the place look much larger than it really is. Over the altar is a picture of a singular construction. It represents clouds with surrounding cherubims, the centre is left open and the light is admitted behind in a particular manner. The nearer you approach the picture the more this middle place seems illuminated. This is said to be an emblem of the deity, tho' I confefs it did not appear a very striking one to me. The latenefs of the hour prevented my examining this picture and the rest of the church as much as I wished.

August 3d

A delay in getting my pafsport has prevented my leaving this place to-day as I intended. I danced attendance, yesterday morning on some *dogs in office* of the municipality and was informed that I must make a request in writing to M^r^ Le Commifsaire Général. This I did before three oclock. I was then told I might call the next morning at 11 oclock and they would *see about it.* I represented that I was to depart the next day and any disappointment would be very embarrafsing.—*Tant pis Monsieur* was the only reply and with this I had to be satisfied. The next morning I went at eleven, had a discription of my face and person taken and was directed to call at three in the afternoon for my pafsport. The dilligence was to sett off at Four and seeing there was a prospect of my being much hurried and fatigued if I persisted in going to day I determined to rest contented till the Dilligence sets off again the day after tomorrow. I was the more willing to do this as Mr Colden & M^r^ S—— had just arrived from Paris having made a hasty tour thro Italy & Switzerland. I have procured considerable information & advice from them that will be useful on my route. S—— is quite tired of travelling, he says he finds himself a little older than when he sat out, but very little wiser. Two thousand Dollars out of pocket and not two thousand cents worth of improvement in. If however he has not acquired much knowledge in his travels he certainly has not fell into that habit of Self importance & affectation common to many young Americans who spend any time in France. If his friends do not find him much better than when he left New York, they will not find him any worse.

Of Mr C—— I can only say he has fully answered the high opinion I had formed of him. He is a gentleman of the worthiest character.

As I am now about quitting Bordeaux it is probably necefsary to say something about its history, its founders, &c, &c. On this subject I shall be very brief for my information is chiefly picked out of French books that I cannot read very fluently.

The historians of Bordeaux make some dispute about its first inhabitants. Two opinions seem to have the most advocates. One is that it was founded by the ancient people of Berry (the Bituriges Vivisci) who fled before Cæsar when he conquered their territory and took refuge in the midst of marshes on the borders of the Garonne where they formed the first rudiments of a town.

The other opinion makes the first settlement more ancient, and ascribes it to a Colony who came from Phénicie in Spain and used to trade among the Gauls. The origin therefore rests in some obscurity and it is of no importance to me to attempt to develope it neither will I dwell upon the etymology of the name which one author thinks derived from the Greek words *Pyrgos* & *Cala* and another from the Latin *Burgus* and *Galate*, both you will perceive have equal claims to credibility, and both are almost as direct & unadulterated derivations as that of *Noah* from *Fohi*.

Under the reign of the Roman Emperor Adrian Bordeaux was established the Metropolis of the second Acquitaine, it was brought to a regular plan and surrounded by walls.

At the Beginning of the fifth century the Visigoths made an irruption for the first time into Gaul, they held pofsefsion of Bordeaux till the commencement of the sixth century when it came under the power of the Kings of France & dukes of Acquitaine.

During this period it was besieged and taken by the Saracens who were in turn defeated by the French. Some of the Dukes who afterwards held pofsefsion of it in common with the rest of the province of Acquitaine endeavored to become absolute masters independent of the King of France. Charlemagne however defeated the last that made the attempt and it is said caused him to be afsafsinated. The city was succefsively ravaged by the Normands the Bretons & the Danes till it was for a while almost abandoned by its former inhabitants.

Some time about the middle of the twelvth century, during the reign of Henry the Second it pafsed into the hands of the English. By these it was held till the year 1453, when it was retaken pofsefsion of by the French who have been masters of it ever since. This is a very brief & perhaps incorrect outline of its history. It has been the seat of many intestine commotions — the object of many battles & sieges. I was shewn a gothic gate with two towers remaining perfect where the civil authorities stood a siege against the populace. Adjoining to this gate is a small church, the door of which is nailed full of horse shoes of different ages and constructions. I was told it had formerly been the custom once a year to form a procefsion to this church and nail a shoe on the door but for why I could not understand. There is a small figure of a horse carved of stone over this door. The gate is of singular construction. Over it is one or two chambers where it is said their parlement used to sit in ancient times. In front of the gate is an old clock & over it a Ball half Black & half gilt that turns upon a pivot & tells the Phazes of the moon.

Bordeaux contains several handsome streets; that of the Chapeau Rouge which leads from the theatre to the Exchange is very handsome. The rue Tourney is also very fine. The Theatre I have already said is a vast superb piece of architecture, there are none in London, Paris in short in Europe to equal it. It is built of the White lime stone used in architecture in Bordeaux. The Port is grand, in form of a crescent, the Buildings in many parts uniform for a great distance and have a noble appearance.

The population of Bordeaux was generally computed at one hundred & twenty or thirty thousand, but it has lately been ascertained that it is not above eighty or ninety thousand. The city has a vast extent along the river, being a compact front of about three miles. It does not however except in the centre run back very far from the river.

The wines of Bordeaux are deservedly of great celebrity and afford a vast article of exportation as do likewise its Brandies. The Canal of Languedoc is of infinite service in facilitating a communication with the Mediterranean. This is the most frequented port in France — particularly by the Americans who really crowded the harbor while I was there.

The Garonne runs by it with extreme rapidity and people are frequently drowned thro carelefsnefs in pafsing among the ships — which are all obliged to anchor in the current there being no built Quay. American seamen are particularly unfortunate in this particular as they often get intoxicated & fall over board where the swiftnefs of the river baffles all their attempts to save themselves. Indeed I myself had a narrow escape from a similar fate one evening. A Vefsel had just arrived from New York and being very anxious to get letters I procured some men to take myself & D Leffingwell of New York, aboard in a Boat. As it was quite dark they could not see far ahead, and run across the cable of a ship. The current set us on so violently that all our efforts to disengage ourselves were for some time ineffectual and we were beginning to prepare to swim for our lives when the men by a violent exertion got us off just as one gunnel of the boat had reached the waters edge & began to ship a sea or two.

Were sufficient care taken in paving Bordeaux, it would be a very agreeable city; but in dry weather the dust is intolerable and in wet weather you are equally annoyed with mud. The people are lively and communicative, but my imperfect knowledge of the language prevented me from mingling among them to advantage—and of observing the particular traits of their characters.

Toulouse. August 8th 1804

I arrived in this city last evening, much fatigued, but highly delighted with my Journey. The country has far exceeded my expectations highly as they were raised, and presented a succefsion of the most beautiful & picturesque scenery. I left Bordeaux on the fifth at four Oclock in the afternoon, in the Dilligence. The company in the carriage consisted of a little opera singer of considerable celebrity her father and mother, a Young French officer, a French gentleman who had just returned from a voyage round the world & myself. The little actrefs belonged to Toulouse and had been to Bordeaux to perform for a few evenings. The young officer was going to Languedoc to see his relations and the voyager to Agen for the same purpose.

The road all the afternoon was sandy and the Country too level to offer much variety. At nine Oclock we stopped at a small town calld Castres, where we supped, after supper we resumed our seats and rode all night. The night was dark and the ride consequently fatiguing. Just before daybreak we crofsed the Garonne at Langon a small town. The Ferriage is by scows, into which the carriages drive the same as those used in America. After crofsing the river we found the road hard and good and the country interesting. We continued riding within sight of the river and just at day break pafsed thro a small village, the inhabitants were still asleep, at one end of the village stood an Old Castle in a very ruinous state. One wing of it however was still standing in tolerable condition. It had a most picturesque appearance as the first gleams of morning fell on its mouldering towers. It stood on the Brow of a high bank of the river, which glittered at its Base. The discriptions of Mrs Radcliffe were brought immediately to my reccollection, this would have formed a fine picture for her talents to work upon. The Dilligence paſsed too fast for me to examine it particularly. After a variety of handsome views rendered particularly so by a charming morning we arrived at the town of Réole, to breakfast. This place was formerly defended by walls & towers. They are now however crumbling away and serve but to give the town a ragged and ancient appearance. There is an old church & convent that formerly belonged to the Benedictines. The manufactures of the town are combs and cutlery.

After Breakfast I exchanged places for the day with a Frenchman who was seated in the *Cabriolet.* This is a place in front of the Dilligence where three persons can sit—it has a boot, like our Gigs & phaetons, and is open in front with an oil cloth curtain to draw in case of rain. It is a little cheaper than the inside of the carriage, but in the summer I think it is preferable as it commands a view of the country round and is cool and agreeable except when the sun is in front. In this place I found a singular little genius, quite an original his name was Henry, a Doctor of Medicine originally of Lancaster in Pennsylvania—by his talk he appears to have been for a long time a citizen of the world. He is about five feet 4 inches high, and thick set, talks French fluently and has an eternal tongue. He knew every body of consequence. Ambassadors, consuls &c were Tom Dick & Harry—intimate acquaintances. The Abby Winkleman had given him a breast pin, Lavater had made him a present of a Snuff Box and several authors had sent him their works to read & criticise. He had been this route before and amused me much by his observations and discriptions. It seems he thought it was necefsary for him to be acquainted with every object of importance we pafsed, to support his character of an intelligent traveller—of course, whenever I enquired respecting any building he had an answer immediately ready, and six times out of ten it was erroneous. A castle he would often mistake for a convent and a manufactory for a church. He however gave me several articles of advice that I expect I shall find useful in travelling. Whenever the Dilligence stopped at any of the small towns to change horses &c we dismounted and strolled thro the streets talking to every one we met. The Voyager could talk English fluently and was much of a Gentleman both in appearance and manners. We found the women very frequently seated outside of their doors at work, and they were always ready to converse. At Tonneins as we were patroling in this manner we pafsed a house where a number of Girls were quilting, we immediately returned and accosted them. I went into the room and one immediately gave me a needle to work with. The girls (in common with the people in this part of France) spoke the language so barbarously that I could not understand what they said. They were highly amused with my bad French, and were laughing the whole time we were there. My companions as I was going away told them I was an *English prisoner* that the young officer had in charge, their merriment immediately gave place to pity, "Ah! le pauvre Garçon," said one to another, "he is merry however, in all his trouble." "And what will they do with him" enquired a young woman of the *Voyager*. "Oh nothing of consequence" replied he — "Perhaps shoot him or cut off his head." The honest souls seemed quite distrefsed for me. I happened to mention that I was thirsty and immediately a bottle of wine was placed before me nor could I prevail on them to take any recompense. In short I departed loaded with their good wishes and I suppose furnished a theme of conversation throughout the village.

After paſsing thro Tonneins and riding a few miles we came to the Banks of the River Lot at which there is a ferry. From this place we had a fine view of Aiguillon a Town situated on an eminence on the opposite side of the river. It had formerly a large chateau belonging to it which was sold as confiscated property in the time of the revolution and part of it has since been demolished, the walls of the town are also in ruins.

Throughout the country we found the people employed in threshing, harvest having been gathered some time before. Threshing seems to be completely a *family* piece of business here and all are employed men women and children. They thresh their grain always in the field, and I have seen eight or nine men & women threshing in one spot, they keep excellent time in their motions, as the safety of their heads depend upon it. The women in this part of the country wear handkerchiefs printed with flowers &c & folded in a particular manner so that a large figure appears on the front of the head & the handkerchief falls down behind with points resembling lace. Fashions seem to be very permanent here, the daughter dreſses like the mother and grandmother and a little distance off you can hardly tell them apart. The masculine labors they go thro in the fields, threshing &c in common with the men, gives them a coarse look and dark complexion directly opposite to beauty and the drefses that they wear, which probably may have been handed down from generation to generation destroy all idea of grace or figure. They however appear to be a gay, contented set of beings that have forgotten that such an idea as *equality* ever existed in France.

At the town of Port St Marie we witnefsed a funeral ceremony of an old man, that was quite new to me. The corps was preceeded by a number of persons habited in white, their faces covered with white veils with two small holes for them to see thro. These I was told, were persons called Penitents, who had made a vow to bury the dead and that they always attended in this drefs with their faces concealed. They were followed by four priests, and then came the corps in an open coffin habited in similar white robes, and the procefsion was closed by the relatives & friends of the deceased. They chanted prayers the whole way and had a most solemn appearance.

We put up at ten oclock at night at Agen a considerable town situated on the Garonne and containing manufactures of silk & woolen. The latenefs of our arrival and our early departure prevented my having an opportunity of viewing the place.

In the morning we set forward at three oclock, & breakfasted at Croquilardit. After leaving this place we continued on for some distance till we arrived at the heights of Moifsac. There I got out and walked up the hills, and never did I see a prospect that gave me more delight. As the road ascended among the heights a continual succefsion of prospects presented themselves. To the right, on an eminence stood the ruins of a castle—the hill on which it was situated gradually swept down into a delightful valley through which the Garonne wandered, giving life & animation to the scene. The hills were covered with Vineyards, and small cottages were scattered in different directions. A number of peasant girls mounted on mules, descending the heights, added to the picturesque nature of the scene. The view from the top of the hill, however, baffles all discription. Beautiful vales presented themselves on every side. The eye embraced a vast extent of country, a vast and firtile valley thro which the Garonne pursued its winding course now lost among the trees that fringed its borders and now breaking upon the view glittering with the sun beams. The country beyond it had the most luxuriant appearance, vineyards, groves & cornfields were mingled together & varied with villages castles & cottages. When I stood upon the height and looked at the enchanting country before me I could not but think of the verses of Watts that you so much admire

Sweet fields beyond the swelling flood
Stand drefsd in living green
So to the Jews old Canaan stood
While Jordan rolld between &c &c

We continued riding among these hills for some time, with the most romantic views continually presenting themselves till we came in sight of the Town of Moifsac. This was situated in a small valley far below us, and before it a small river pafsed rapidly along. As we wound down the hill the town was seen in different directions and its old towers and battlements had a fine effect from the situation in which they were placed. After crofsing the ferry at this town we found ourselves on one of the vast plains of Languedoc. We were the whole afternoon crofsing it. The harvest had lately been gathered so that the plain had not a very verdant appearance. It was sun set when we arrived at this place which is situated at one extremity of the plain, and is built on both sides of the Garonne. As I am tired of discription and it is late at night you must excuse anything very particular about this place. It is by no means to compare with Bordeaux for beauty, tho it has several beautiful walks in its environs. It is built entirely of Brick, and the Brick is by no means so handsomely manufactured or so handsomely put together as the Brick in New York. The streets are very narrow & winding. I have been in two or three of the churches which were profusely adorned with pictures & paintings.

The Theatre is a shabby old building—you approach to it thro a convent or rather what *was* a convent. The interior of the Theatre is equally poor and the scenery old & tarnished. It is lighted the same way as all the French theatres that I have seen, are, by a chandalier hung in the centre & by the lamps ranged along the front of the stage as with us.

The Capitoul, or City Hall of Toulouse is a handsome building & occupies one side of a tolerable square. There is a handsome Bridge over the Garonne which commands a fine view up & down the river, with a distant prospect of the Lofty Pyrenees the mountains that divide France from Spain.

The Esplanade along the Banks of the Garonne and other walks in the environs of the town are very handfome.

This place was formerly a Capital of the Visigoths and has been the seat of many commotions. The Young French officer was very attentive and polite in shewing me the place — he had been here before and was acquainted with the streets &c.

The next morning (9th) I took paſsage on board of a post boat of the canal of Languedoc. I found on board the Little Doctor, whom I mentioned before, and a young midshipman who had come by the same Dilligence with me and was going to join his ship at Toulon.

The Post boat is drawn by two horses and goes at the rate of ten or twelve leagues a day. The locks are very numerous and every now and then the Baggage was shifted from one boat into another which caused considerable delay. The boats have cabins of nearly their whole length and high enough for a tall man to walk upright in them. The canal winded thro the most delightful plains highly cultivated; the hills gentlely swelling & crowned with villages & castles. There is vast quantities of Indian corn raised in these plains, which almost made me fancy myself in my own country.

There were two very pretty French girls on board, to whom the little Doctor (who among his other qualities poſseſses a world of Galantry) was exceeding attentive and officious. In the afternoon they were leaving the boat to go to their homes in a neighboring town. The Doctor would not let them go without a great many compliments & kept us waiting by his talk. At last as one of the Girls attempted to get away from him he seized her by the gown, she pulled off his hat with his peruque in it, he chased her and she threw the wig into the canal. It was a high scene to see the little man fishing for his wig bald headed.

The canal throughout, paſsed thro a variety of the most beautiful scenery. At one time it was higher than the adjacent plain and wound round a bluff of land on which were the ruins of an old castle while below the plain presented a scene of mingled verdures with a beautiful river winding through it. The same river after a while rolls *under* the canal which is conducted over it in an arched aqueduct of stone. It then meanders thro the valley to the right and is lost among distant Hills. At another time it paſsed by the walls of an old town built on the side of a Hill the old towers of which formed picturesque objects in the extensive prospect. The sunsets were particularly beautiful. At one place where we put up for the night I was delighted with an evening promenade. It was one of those mild lovely evenings common in this Delightful country. The Sun sunk behind the distant Hills shedding rays of the mildest glory on the surrounding country. A rich yellow gleam was cast upon the mouldring towers of Trèbes, (the small town where I put up). The distant hills were tinged with the softest blues & purples and the mistiness of evening blended the valleys into the utmost harmony of tone softening every harsh & discordant feature or color of the landscape and producing a tout ensemble the most mild & enchanting.

The canal at one time pafses under a hill, the pafs is called the *Montagne Percée* It is said to be four hundred & eighty feet in length—is handsomely arched & part of the way with hewn stone. On the top of the hill are Vineyards & cornfields.

The Auberges (Inns) at which you stop in going by the Canal are very poor and the people not very attentive. At one of them where we stopped to dine I met an American gentleman & his lady who were making a tour in France. You should be in my situation, solitary & among strangers of a different country language & manners to conceive my pleasure at encountering Americans so unexpectedly. Dinner time pafsed away most rapidly & agreeably. The Lady was handsome & engaging and her husband a very clever fellow. They were of Boston. It was with the utmost regret I parted with them.

The Peasantry are a coarse rugged set of beings, some of the men have exceeding sunburnt complexions & black hair and look something like our

Indians. The Women are sturdy masculine and most disgusting viragos. They are continually scolding and bawl out with the utmost rapidity and violence, accompanying their vulgar & indecent language with distortions and furious gesticulations. At one time as I was walking along the banks of the canal I took the liberty of gathering some figs from a tree near a house. One of these termagents immediately attacked me with her tongue demanding money for what I had taken; & scolding most horridly—I stood patiently and every time she stopped to take breath shrugged up my shoulders & said *Nong tong paw.* She at last had to give out & left me cursing me for *un misérable anglais.*

At all the towns we pafsed that were situated near the canal there were great numbers of the women standing in the water washing clothes. This is done by laying the clothes on a rough stone & beating them with a flat piece of board—a manner eminently calculated to benefit the linen manufactories. There appeared a great scarcity of Petticoats among these women one petticoat having often apparently been divided among two or three of them. The Drefs of the women is very grotesque—a long waist, red petticoat and woolen hat with a round crown & enormous brim. I generally made my breakfast on bread wine & grapes, in the boat in preference to stopping at the dirty auberges.

After three days & a half sailing on the canal amid a variety of scenery similar to what I have described we arrived at Béziers. This town is finely situated on a hill and appears very handsome from a distance. The cathedral & a convent are very conspicuous & the former is a handsome old building. You approach the town over a beautiful stone bridge of several arches that crofses the river Orbe. A road is cut in a zig zag direction up the side of the Hill and enters one of the gates at the Highest part of the town. From this road you have a grand & extensive view. At your feet are the suburbs of the city by which pafses the beautiful river Orbe, running thro a vally the most fruitful & highly cultivated, distributed into vineyards, corn fields & plantations of olives & almonds and high mountains in the distance.

I had not time to examine this handsome little town as much as I wished, as I was to set off immediately after dinner on the route to Montpellier. The Doctor had agreed with the owner of a Berlin to take the young midshipman & myself to that place. The owner at first demanded eighteen livres from each of us, but the Doctor who is an old traveller made him take that sum for *both*—an instance of the extortion of these people. The Little D^{r} I found a most excellent hand to manage these affairs, so that when any demand was made upon me I pretended not to understand & turned them over to the Doctor — by this means I escaped much trouble and imposition & the D^{r} was highly pleased with his employment. I was particularly amused with a scene between him and a woman who owned a cart that had brought our trunks from the canal to the inn. She demanded three times her due. The Doctor refused to give her a farthing more than the just price. A violent contest ensued, the D^{r} pretended to be in a violent paſsion, and fairly outdid her in talk & gesticulation, so that she was obliged to put up with the price he chose to give. The poor woman when she found that she could not get in a word edge ways began to cry & afterwards swore that if that little man had not have talked so much & so fast she would have had twice as much.

The Doctor took a place in the Berlin with us, as far as Mèze, a small town on the coast of the Mediteranian The owner of the Berlin had engaged to have three mules but when we came to set off he had but two. He seemed out of humor from the Doctors having obliged him to make an honest bargain We were dragged along at a snails pace for the driver would not put his mules off of a walk. In the evening we put up at Pézenas, a handsome little town with pleasant walks in its environs. Took an agreeable evening promenade.

The next morning (13th) we rose early & resumed our route. The day break was beautiful. The similar scenery as the preceding—vineyards olives, almonds & mulberrys, &c. After sun rize we arrived on an eminence and for the first time I had a sight of the Mediteranean. The prospect was superb. A vast extent of country lay before me presenting a perfect paradise and beyond it the Mediterranean was seen, smooth and unruffled, with numbers of fishing boats reposing on its bosom. The sun had just gained a little height and cast a gleam of splendor on the glafsy ocean. We breakfasted at Mèze a small town beautifully situated on the sea shore, & here we parted with the little Doctor who intended taking a fishing boat there to go to Cette a small sea port. It was with regret I took leave of the little man for he had proved a most amusing character to me. He is an excentric genius, with a great deal of talk & considerable information. He pofsefses the happy faculty of making himself at home every where has something to say to every body & is acquainted with any person in five minutes. He has a great flow of spirits much drollery

& is very fond of quizzing. He was continually paſs-ing himself off on the Peasants for a variety of char-acters—Sometimes a Swede, sometimes a Turk, now a German & now a Dutchman. With a Farmer he was a wine merchant, with a shoemaker, a Tanner, with an officer he was a former captain in the American Army with others a profeſsor in one of the German Colleges & with others a Sec-retary of the American Minister who was travel-ling with dispatches to Commodore Preble in the Mediteranean. He talked four or five languages, told the honest people wonderful stories of his hair breadth scapes among the Turks & the American Indians.

In one town he made them believe I was an English prisoner, in another he took the landlady aside told her I was a young Mameluke of distinc-tion travelling *incog* & that he was my interpreter, asked her to bring me a large chair that I might sit croſs legged after the manner of my country and desired a long pipe for me that I might smoke — perfumes. The good woman believed every word, said she had no large chair but she could place two chairs for me and as to a pipe she had none longer than was generally used by the country people. The doctor said that would not do and since she could not furnish those articles she might bring a bottle of her best wine with good bread & cheese & we would eat breakfast.

He gave me a variety of servicable advice concerning travelling, and bade me good bye telling me when next we met I might probably find him a conjurer or high German Doctor.

After riding thro a variety of charming views with the Mediterranian frequently presenting itself, we arrived at five oclock at Montpelier.

Here we had no sooner stopped than I was assaild by a regiment of porters, voituriers & servants. Some wanted my trunk, others to know if I wanted a voiture for any other town & others reccommending their several hotels. I repaired to the Hotel du Midi—My trunk was brought to my room by *two* porters one of whom I amply paid, the other insisted on a gratuity & was so clamorous that I had to bundle him head & heels out of the door and slammed it to telling him to go & divide the *spoils* with his brother vagabond.

Montpellier, [*August*] 15th

Montpellier is said to contain about 30,000 Inhabitants. It is pleasantly situated on an eminence, by which it enjoys a free circulation of air & of the sea Breezes. The streets however in the interior, like those of all the French towns I have seen, are very narrow and winding and extremely dirty. The police of the place seem very inattentive to promoting its cleanlinefs, which, considering it as the resort of so many invalids, I should think ought to be an object of the first attention. The exterior of the city is handfome, particularly the western side. The walls are old but picturesque & there is a very fine gate on that side.

The walks in the environs of the city are extremely pleasant & command fine prospects. One in particular is superb, called *La place de Peyrou*. This is a fine extensive terrace surrounded with handsome stone ballustrades, at one end is a Beautiful Temple built of white stone with pillars of the Corinthian order. In the middle of it is a fountain of the most limpid water that diffuses a delightful coolnefs around. Before the temple is a fish pond of the same clear water, tolerably stocked with fish. A grand aqueduct of stone resembling two bridges, one on top of the other, crofses a valley from a hill at a considerable distance and communicates with the terrace in rear of the temple. This aqueduct convoys the water that supplies the town. The lower part of the Aqueduct has about 50 arches, the upper part, nearly three times the number but smaller. The squares & places in the city are decorated with very handsome fountains surmounted with statues &c.

The view from the Place de Peyrou is extensive and beautiful. You have before you a vast & enchanting plain terminated on one side by Mountains and on the other by the Mediterranean. On a clear day you can see from this place, the Alps in one direction & the Pyrenees in an opposite, both at a vast distance.

The theatre is a decent looking building outside, and the interior is finished with much taste and prettineſs. It is nearly about the size of our theatre at New York, but the stage is much smaller. The scenery is but indifferent, they have not in any theatre that I have seen in France the facility of shifting the scenery that you observe in our theatre. A scene always stands a whole act & is not shifted till the curtain is down. One of the pieces they were acting in this Theatre when I was there, was a Melodrame, a species of play that is very fashionable at present in Paris. At the conclusion of the piece a crown of laurel was thrown on the stage to a favorite actreſs who had distinguished herself that evening. This is a testimony of high approbation, common in France and when I was at Bordeaux La Fond the famous Actor had two thrown to him in the course of one evening.

On returning last night to the Inn, I was surprised & pleased at finding the Little Doctor there. He had dispatched his busineſs at Cette and intended going on to Nice, where he should remain some time for his health. He introduced me this morning to a Mr Walsh of this place, originally an Irishman, but a naturalized citizen of America. He gave us the most open & hospitable reception, and insisted on our dining with him. The afternoon paſsed most agreeably as the honest hearty welcome of this clever fellow made us perfectly at home in his company.

This day has been the fête of the Aſsumption. In the evening I was attracted by a crowd & the sound of music, to one of the principal streets. I found a company of Bakers, who were celebrating the holiday with their sweethearts. The men were dreſsed in pink Jackets & white pantaloons with a sash round their waists and large cocked hats with enormous bunches of colored feathers. The girls wore yellow boddices & white petticoats and a little yellow hat stuck on one side of their heads gave them a very smart & coquetish appearance, they all held garlands of flowers & were dancing to the music of two or three Savoyards. This is a specimen of the livelineſs & gaiety of heart that characterized this people before the revolution, but which I am told has disappeared considerably since. To me however, who did not know them in their most thoughtlefs days, they still appear all vivacity and affability. This fête of Afsumption I am told is celebrated with procefsions &c in other places, but those are not permitted in towns like Montpellier where a great part of the inhabitants are Protestants.

I saw more pretty faces in proportion among the girls of Montpellier than I have seen in any place in France besides. The climate of this place is said to have altered much for the worse in late years, the Spring & summer are very variable—all the while of my stay it was extremely hot. Autumn is the most favorable season.

[*August*] 16th

I set off in company with the Doctor early this morning for Nismes, in a Voiture, between Montpellier and Lunel we met with four conscripts in chains, guarded by two soldiers on horseback. The conscripts are young men who at a certain age are obliged to join the Army, and as they sometimes are reluctant to leave their family & friends they are conducted to their regiment in chains & sometimes imprisoned to prevent their escaping.

We dined at Lunel, a small town famous for its white wines. Here I was amused by a quarrel between two upright Postillions who were disputing which was the greatest rogue. One charged the other with stealing from the travellers, he retorted in turn and charged the other with stealing from the travellers & his master into the bargain.

"*When Greek meets Greek then comes the tug of War.*"

We entered Nismes this evening and Drove thro a public place where they were celebrating the Fair of St Roque. Above all afsemblages of Discordant noises that I have ever heard, I place a French fair without hesitation.

Drums & trumpets of Shewmen & jugglers, Whistles & pipes of children braying of Jackafses and as to the clack & confusion of womens' tongues, the tower of Babel itself could not have presented a more confused chattering.

[*August*] 17th

The fair is over, to day, but the sound of it is still to be heard. It has supplied all the children in the town with Drums trumpets and whistles and the whole place resounds with them. This was but a trifling fair, but I am told that some of the principal ones, held at large towns and at stated periods, are vast and extremely curious. Had Hogarth ever been present at one of them he would have found an excellent situation for his *enraged Musician*.

Nismes is placed by some historians 580 Years before Rome and in antient time was a city of great consequence. The inhabitants at present are said to be 40,000. Judging from the size of the place I should not think there were above half the number, but the houses are large and the French have a great faculty of stowing and packing their carcafses in a very small space so that one of their houses would almost people a dozen in America. There are a number of Roman Antiquities in this place in good preservation.

The Ampitheatre is a grand ruin and said to be the most perfect one of the kind in France. It is an elipse the grand axis of which is 67 Toises, 3 feet and the smaller 52 toises, 5 feet. It has a noble appearance, outside, though much ruined and disfigured. The lower part supposed to have been built in the reign of Antoninus Pius consists of sixty arcades that run round the building and formerly opened into a Piazza. The upper Story is of the same number of arcades tho the Pillars are of a Different order. Several ranges of seats still remain on the inside, they are oblong stones of six or eight feet in Length and about two in diameter; and offer a striking contrast to the modern luxury of stuffed seats & leaning places. I believe there was no cement or mortar used in erecting the walls of this immense building. There is mortar at present in several places but it seems to have been put there in more modern times to prevent the places from giving way. The surfaces of the stone where they touch each other are cut very even so as to fit well & to be compact—in many of the highest parts of the walls I saw vast stones of eighteen feet in length. The Romans must have had some immense & powerful machine to raise these enormous stones the height of above sixty feet from the ground, and to place them in particular situations, besides, they must have been able to raise them with facility, otherwise they would certainly have prepared smaller stones which were more portable. The Ampitheatre has suffered more from Sieges & fire than from the gradual delapidations of time. Its injuries bear the marks of force and violence rather than the crumbling appearance of decay. It served as a fortreſs to the Saracens and sustained many aſsaults. To prevent them from again applying it to that use Charles Martel is said to have filled it with faggots to which he set fire in hopes of destroying it. The flames have blackened the walls outside, but the materials were not sufficiently inflammable to be consumed. The Arena is crowded with shabby houses of poor people, they have also turned the arcades of the lower story outside into Botiques and Dram Shops which prevents the curious examiner from seeing a great part of the construction.

In 1780 the King gave orders to demolish these houses and to put the edifice as nearly as poſsible into its original state. These orders however were never put in execution for the houses still stand there a matter of grievance to every antiquarian.

P.S. It is computed to have been able to contain 17,000 spectators at 20 inches each.

The Maison Carrée is the most perfect Roman remain I have yet seen, and is spoken of by French artists in the highest manner for the beauty of its proportions and the perfect manner in which it is finished. It is 82 feet long 35 feet Broad & 37 high, oblong and decorated with columns of the Corinthian order. It is a temple that was consecrated to Caius & Lucius Caesar, adopted sons of Augustus. The frize and cornice are sculptured in a very delicate taste. The other chief Antiquities are the *Tour Magne* supposed to have formerly been a pharos much ruined at present, the ruins of a temple of Diana, a Roman gate & two Mosaic pavements.

The Fountain of Nismes is superb. What is termed the fountain itself runs near the temple of Diana and supplies the whole City with water. But there is a garden near the fountain, which is called by that name, adorned with canals and various water works, erected over the vestiges of some Antient Roman Baths. These works are of hewn stone, ornamented with Statues &c. and are objects both of curiosity and admiration.

The Streets of Nismes are remarkably dusty. The Dust is very light and the least breeze of wind carries it along in clouds. The Manufactories of Nismes are silks, silk stockings & some woolens.

A Roman Colony was settled at Nismes by Marcus Agrippa son in law of Augustus.

By some conversation I had with D[r] Henry I had got quite out of conceit of my American protection, it was in writing from the Mayor of New York and he said it was a chance if any of the French officers of Police would be able to read it or would know whether to give credence to the signature of the Mayor or not.

My French pafsport also gave a very poor discription of me, and as I was continually mistaken on the road for an Englishman, I began to apprehend I might get into some disagreeable situation with the police before I could reach Marseilles. I was much startled therefore at Nismes while sitting at supper with several others in the hotel, at the entry of two or three officers of the police with a file of soldiers. They only came however to examine our paſsports and they paſsd over mine very lightly. A Young Frenchman present was very impertinent to them, knowing that he had a sufficient paſsport in his pocket. The officers got highly enraged threatened him with arrest, and one little fellow seemed ready to jump over the table at him. They had, however, a stubborn fellow to manage, for he laughed at their menaces and amused himself with their paſsionate expreſsions.

At Nismes I parted once more with the little Doctor, who was so unwell that he could not proceed. He intended to return to Montpellier and endeavor to proceed from Cette by water.

I have been two or three times more to look at the *Maison Carrée* and cannot sufficiently admire the sweetneſs of its construction and the exquisite taste with which it is finished.

August 19th

I left Nismes in the Dilligence for Avignon. After riding two posts we came to the small river LaFoux, on the opposite side of which was situated the small town of the same name, having a very picturesque appearance. We croſsed the ferry and then the country began to change and become more mountainous. We ascended among the heights and rode the most of the afternoon along a ridge of high rocky hills from whence we had now and then, delightful prospects of the Distant valleys offering a charming prospect of verdure & fertility to the rugged barrenneſs of the mountains. Towards Sun set we came to where the road descended from the heights, and the View that here broke upon us surpaſsed every landscape I had seen in France. At the foot of the hill lay the town of Villeneuve thrown in shade by the hill excepting an antient convent of Chartreuse formerly of great wealth & grandeur. This stood on an eminence high above the rest of the town, and the rich gleams of the setting sun, cast upon its towers & battlements of Yellowish Stone, rendered it a prominent and interesting object. At a small distance were seen the antient towers & castle of Avignon half buried in trees that are planted round the outside of the walls and reflected in the Rhone that paſses rapidly by. These towns are situated in one of those enchanting valleys that I have already described, where nature seems to have exerted herself particularly to harmonize the scene and to fit it for the abode of tranquility & Love. The valley is highly cultivated, the Rhone wanders irregularly thro it and is seen to a vast distance forming delightful islands of luxurient fertility. The view is bounded by ridges of Mountains. When I saw it the sun was setting among clouds and here & there threw partial gleams of the mildest radiance on the landscape in one place lignung up the walls of an old tower, in another resting in rich refulgence on a Distant mountain while the others were enveloped in the shades of evening. After descending from the heights we entered the town of Villeneuve where we quit the Dilligence and left our trunks to be carried to the Bureau of the Port at Avignon, we then walked to the ferry which was at some distance, where we crofsed the Rhone in a scow; on the opposite side we landed under the walls of Avignon. In our way to the gate of the city we pafsed under a high cliff, on which is situated the castle in which the popes formerly resided. On top on an old tower or rampart on the brow of the cliff, were seated two soldiers, enjoying the setting sun and playing on a French horn & clarionet. Their Situation, appearance and music was very interesting & seemed to accord with the romantic Scenery around.

[*August*] 20th

Avignon is celebrated in the classic world, for having been the residence of Petrarch and Laura. I was shewn a picture in the portico of the Church *de Notre Dame de Don*, of St George Slaying the Dragon and before him a Lady Kneeling in an attitude of Supplication. This is said to be intended for a representation of Petrarch & Laura, the likenefs of the former being taken in St George & of the latter in the lady. The painting is so much defaced by time that the countenances & part of the figures are not discernable. The interior of this church was finished in an exquisite taste with carvings, gildings, paintings, reliefs &c and has been admired by the most celebrated masters. The blind fury of the revolutionary mobs has stripped it of its paintings and scatterd the fine carvings &c in fragments about the floor. The church however is still magnificent, in ruins, & worthy the attention of the traveller. The same rash & indiscriminating fanaticism that destroyed this beautiful edifice, has also entirely demolished the church of the Cordeliers which contained the tomb of the fair Laura, so that there is no vestige remaining.

Avignon was antiently held by the Romans, after the destruction of the Empire it went thro many changes and masters. In 1348 it was sold by Joan Queen of Naples to the pope, after she had lost her crown & been driven out of Italy. For seventy two years this was the seat of the popes till Gregory XI restored that honor to the Vatican. It is said to contain between twenty & thirty thousand Inhabitants. It formerly boasted a vast number of churches & convents, the bells of which kept a continual jingling which occasioned Rabelais to give it the name of the *Isle sonnante*. Many of these churches still remain, but in a ruinous situation. I observed in most of the towns thro which I have paſsed, that they are endeavoring to repair the churches & once more put them in a State for worship. This is by order of Bonaparte who is rapidly reestablishing the papal religion. It will be impossible for them however to replace the fine Gothic ornaments the superb paintings & carvings that their senseleſs fury has demolished.

In Avignon was stationed a troop of Gens d'armes. Their horses were the finest that I have seen in France, but the vagabonds do not seem to know how to treat them. I saw one of them cleaning his horse at the Door of the Gendarmerie. It was a beautiful animal & full of spirits. As he was combing it, the horse started. The brute flew in a violent paſsion to chastise the horse, threw large stones at him sufficient to break his ribs and maim him forever. This cruelty to horses is universal among the lower order of French. I have seen a postillion exercise a continual flagellation on two or three poor skeletons of horses from the time they set out from the post house till they arrived at the place of relay. One fellow in particular between Bordeaux & Toulouse, had four poor Animals before the dilligence who had been so constantly used that their flesh was raw wherever it touched the traces, they were lame sick & weary. This however excited no indulgence in the wretch who drove them, he flogged them the more, to make them dread the pain of the whip more than of their sores. At the end of the post he came with hat in hand, to beg the customary gratuity given to postillions. I ordered him away & told him such a cruel scoundrel as himself deserved to be put in the horses place and made to feel a little of his own discipline. The other paſsengers likewise refused to give him anything, and I believe he got a leſson that made more impreſsion than any he had ever received as it was addreſsed not to his heart — but to his *pocket*.

I have heard it remarked by some traveller that when you set off in any town in France, you must calculate on at least three or four stops before you get out of the town. Some part of the harneſs gives way, or some buckle is displaced or some strap is out of order. This is an absolute fact. For my part I generally allow two stops to a league and find on an average I am tolerably correct. The French load their horses with a huge quantity of Leather wood braſs and iron. An immense ſtuffd & peaked yoke is placed upon their necks and then their whole carcafs is covered with straps saddles belts &c studded with brafs nails, ornamented with worsted bobs and a profusion of bells that give a most harmonious sound. As these harnefses are of Antient date and may have probably flourished for one or two centuries, you may suppose they are not of the strongest texture. They are however, mended with pieces of rope thongs of leather &c &c and it is natural to suppose that a machine so complicated, that depends upon so many minute articles to keep it together, must frequently get out of order.

But to return, to Avignon. On an eminence at one end of the town stands the castle in which the popes formerly resided. It is a venerable looking old building & very large. Above it is an esplanade on top of the hill from whence the prospect is superb. I was up there at sun rise and took the same stand where I had seen the two soldiers the preceding evening. It commanded a considerable view of, the town—the walls flanked with square towers that surrounded it, the beautiful walks in the environs, and the rich & fertile valley stretching to a vast extent, with the Rhone winding in glittering splendor thro it. At a distance was the town of Villeneuve with the old convent of Chartreuse. Below me were boatmen fishermen &c in groups on the shore joking & laughing tho their voices were almost lost in distance; three or four arches of an old bridge, that stood in the river with an Antique tower on them added to the picturesque beauties around me. The air was pure salubrious & reviving and I do not know when I have enjoyed a prospect more exquisitely than at this time.

For Beauty of situation and surrounding scenery Avignon is worthy of having been the residence of so celebrated a poet. The variegated lovelineſs of the neighboring country is enough to enliven the mind and call forth all the native powers of poetry. It appears to me that Avignon would prove a most favorable residence for the valitudinarian in regard to beauty of Landscape and pleasant walks tho I am unacquainted to what degree the climate is beneficial in this particular spot.

Marseilles, [*August*] 22^{d}

I arrived in this city last evening after a tiresome ride of twenty-two hours from Avignon. In our way we stopped to dine at Aix, a handsome town with wide clean streets and agreeable public walks. This was a Parliament town under the former Government. It is often resorted to by invalids on account of its mineral baths which were celebrated in time of the Romans and lost till the beginning of the last century when they were discovered in digging for the foundation of an Edifice without the city walls. We did not rest long enough in the town to allow me to examine its buildings or curiosities.

The new city (or rather the new *part*) of Marseilles is well built, the streets regular clean well paved and wide. The old part of the city is villainously filthy, the streets narrow and crooked. They have fountains that play in different parts of the city and supply streams of water thrō many of the streets, yet it is impoſsible to carry off the vile smells that prevail throughout the place in consequence of all filth & dirt being thrown into the streets. With all its beauty therefore, Marseilles is a disagreeable place for an invalid to reside at, who is peculiarly sensible to corrupt air.

The port of Marseilles is excellently contrived to ensure the safety of Veſsels, it is oblong with a narrow entrance defended by a fort on each side. The Quay is well paved with bricks laid edgeways, and for the width of two feet next the water, it is paved with square stones. It is amusing to walk on this quay and see the variety of beings aſsembled together of different nations languages & dreſses. The Tunisians, Algerines Spaniards Genoese, Italians & French all mingled together, form a curious medley.

[*August*] 25th

There are but two American Veſsels in port, at present. This somewhat surprized me, as Marseilles is most favorably situated for enjoying & almost engroſsing the trade of the Mediterranean. But I am told that the restrictions laid on commerce by duties &c, the impositions & delays of the Custom House & many other inconveniences are rapidly discouraging all trade with this port and induce the Americans to go to Leghorn in preference, as there they are leſs annoyed & impeded in their trade. Many petitions and complaints have been made to the Government on this head by the Merchants of Marseilles, but the Government is too much engaged in planning victories at present as to attend to such a dull mechanical inglorious affair as commerce. The taxes and duties are enormous and more felt in Marseilles than in most ports, insomuch that several of the oldest houses have abandoned busineſs rather than be subject to them.

I have met with a very agreeable companion here, in a Mr Appleton, a young gentleman of Boston who came out supercargo of a Brig which he has sent to Naples and awaits her return. He is a young fellow of an excellent disposition good understanding and most amiable manners. After paſsing thro a considerable tract of country among strangers of a different language & nation you cannot imagine how grateful it is to encounter a fellow countryman. The heart hails him as a Brother to whom it is entitled to look for friendship.

[*August*] 27th

I was agreeably surprized the other evening on returning to the hotel from a promenade, to find Dr Henry quietly seated in the parlor. It seemd as if the little man had dropped from the clouds, for I had supposed him still at Cette. He told me he had reached there the day he parted with me at Nismes but found that no veſsel would sail in leſs than two Months, as they would not have a convoy before that time. His complaint encreasing he determined once more to try the Journey by land and after divers misfortunes, the carriage overturning &c he arrived safe at Marseilles. His health is better at present, his spirits have returned and he is again as merry as a cricket.

The Theatre of Marseilles is a neat building of white stone. I went there to see for the first time a French ballet. The Dancing was admirable, but the immodesty of the women who danced rather offended my old fashioned, American ideas of propriety.

As to the French style of Acting, it is contrary

to all that I have been accustomed to admire. It appears to me a continual violation of Nature, affected positions, strained attitudes, violent and uncouth gestures, and excefsive ranting. In their dancing, fighting &c they keep excellent time to the music, and are very graceful, of course they are good in pantomine, and, till I get more accustomed to their style of acting, or better acquainted with their language, that is the only species of entertainment in which I can be much pleased with them. I must however do them the justice to say that the singing parts of their operas are sometimes very well performed.

Marseilles, like all the other French towns is thronged with beggars. This is a natural consequence of the discouragements & checks Commerce has received. I believe the Americans are generally considered the patrons of beggars shoe blacks fiddlers & pedlars, for never were mortals so harrafsed with them as we are at the hotel where I lodge & where all the Americans that come to Marseilles, reside. We can seldom go out but we are escorted by a regiment of ragged boys, who have a knack of rattling off a tune by drumming with both fists on the chin, this causes the mouth to open quick with a peculiar sound & very loud. Our doors are besieged by singing beggars and pedlars with their gilded trumpery, and the shoe blacks thinking to gain our custom by speaking English, run after us in the street with their brushes & blacking crying "Monsieur, monsieur, G—d dam, G—d dam son de bish son de bish."

September 3[d]

I HAD anticipated some amusement at the Fair of S[t] Lazare which commenced last week & which I had heard some talk of before. It is however, but a paltry affair, merely calculated for poor people and children. At some of the French fairs where they vend silks and other valuable merchandizes there is generally a vast concourse of people, and great sums of money are expended. Here the articles of trade were chiefly toys & tin ware, with here and there a little vampd up jewelry. In one stall the owner had a little of every thing collected and sold his articles indiscriminately at twenty eight sous apiece. I have seen very few shew men & no jugglers at this fair, but I expect they do not exhibit much till the last days. Yesterday afternoon Blanchard (the Aereal navigator who once made an unsuccefsful attempt in New York) took a flight in a balloon from a plain in an elevated part of the suburbs. He had prepared the public mind by flaming handbills, announcing that himself & his wife would go up in a great balloon to which would be attached two smaller ones. Of course all the good people of Marseilles repaired to the hills & high places to see the wonder, and had the enemy been nigh they might have played the same trick that Yorick relates happened to Strafsburg "that the enemy marched in at one end of the town as the Citizens marched out of the other."

The streets that led to the plain were barricaded and guarded by soldiers, the tickets of admifsion were thirty sous. Blanchard had very wisely sold his day's profits to some officers of the police for six thousand Livres by which the worthy souls "gained a lofs" of about two or three thousand, for though the people of Marseilles were all very willing to see the ascension yet but a small proportion were inclined to spend thirty sous upon their curiosity.

The ascension took place, to be sure, but with the trifling variation from the bill, that there was but one balloon instead of three, that it was much smaller than they expected, and not above two thirds filled, that Mr Blanchard went up *solus*, that he ascended to a very inconsiderable height and descended about a mile from the place he started, so that the people one and all with their accustomed ease and politenefs pronounced Mr Blanchard "a f—— and sent him to the d—l."

On the plain we encountered the American Consul Mr Cathalin and his lady, and a young fellow who is some relation to him and acts as his chancellor. I have neglected to mention these geniuses before, which is almost unpardonable for they have afforded us a vast deal of amusement at the hotel where I reside. Cathalin is a small man — a Frenchman but talks English fluently.

[*September*] 8th

I was to the theatre the other evening to see for the first time a French ballet. The Scenery, drefses &c were very good, and the dancers delighted me from the beauty and agility of their steps and the elegance of their attitudes. The Women were drefsed in a flesh colored habit fitted exactly to their Shapes so that it really looked like the Skin, over this was a light robe of white muslin ornamented very tastily but so transparent that their figures were perfectly visible through it and in dancing particularly were completely exposed. As I was unaccustomed to see women expose themselves thus publicly I felt my American blood mounting in my cheeks on their account and would have been happy to have given them another petticoat or a thicker robe to cover their nakednefs. The Audience seemed to look on with perfect indifference not perceiving any thing immodest or improper in it and the ladies regarded with perfect indifference a Spectacle at which our American girls could not even peep thro their fans without blushing. These lascivious exhibitions are strong evidences of the depraved morals and licentiousnefs of the public. The Stage which should be employed by "holding the mirror up to nature" to inform the understanding and improve the heart is degraded by performances devoted to sensuality and libertinism.

I have seen no stage in France that I think equals ours in the management of the scenery machinery & other parts of the stage businefs. The grand theatre at Bordeaux, it is true, did not exhibit much change of scenery while I was there so that I had not sufficient opportunity to judge well of its stage management.

[*September*] 9th

The ascension of Mr Blanchard has introduced a new *play thing* among the *grown children* of Marseilles. The Balloon Mania has absolutely arisen to an alarming height. Paper balloons are sent up from different parts of the town & from the country seats adjacent every day. This day being Sunday & of course a *holiday* in France they have full opportunity to indulge in all the pleasures of *gas & steel filings.* I have counted this afternoon four air balloons up above the City at one time & some of them quite large. The whole town is crazy after them. Happy people—"Pleased with a feather—tickled with a straw," you forget your national calamities at the sight of any new amusement however trifling.

There are two pleasant walks at Marseilles, one thro the centre of the town shaded with fine large trees and the houses on each side well built, the other at one end ascending a hill called Mount Bonaparte. In the evenings and on Sundays they are much frequented. The manufactures of Marseilles are gold & silver stuffs laces silk stockings Woolens and they export much wine oil and wool. The climate during my stay was very hot, (as it is all summer) but the sea breezes were often refreshing. The Valley in which Marseilles is situated is well cultivated and crowded with country seats & gardens.

The Marseillians date the origen of their city from a Colony of Phocians, who, they say, founded it about six hundred years before the birth of our Saviour. It has some celebrity from the friendship it shewed for Pompey & its strenuous opposition to Caesar. The latter when on his way to Spain to oppose the friends of Pompey, wished to enter Marseilles but the inhabitants resolutely shut their gates against him. Enraged at this conduct he immediately invested it by sea and land and shortly after departed to prosecute his designs in Spain, leaving the seige under the direction of Trebonius and Decimus Brutus.

The Situation of Marseilles must have been different in those days from its present one as it is said to have been "covered on three sides by water & on the fourth only accefsible by an isthmus or neck of land" (vide Ferg. Rom. Rep.) & this Isthmus was defended by high walls & towers. The Marseillans were enspirited by the presence of Domitius, a Roman pro consul, and expected speedy release from Pompey; they were therefore uncommonly persevering & courageous in defence of their city frequently making sallies & burning the works of the besiegers. They had particular engines of extraordinary force with which they discharged arrows or rather beams of wood twelve feet long and proportionately thick which penetrated the works of the besiegers and obliged them to redouble the force of their skreens & walls.

When the town was reduced to the last extremity Caesar arrived, accepted their offers of capitulation & took pofsefsion of the city treating the inhabitants with great mildnefs & indulgence.

September 10th

This morning I left Marseilles in Company with Dr H., we having engaged a Voiture to carry us to Nice. We sat off at day break and took a crofs road that was in the evening to join the main road from Aix to Nice. The country thro which we pafsed in the morning was hilly and sterile and cultivated by the afsistance of Manure. We rode thro the small town of Creal; this had formerly been absolutely a horde of Banditti. The People of the Fauxbourgs (suburbs) began by plundering the houses of the Richer citizens after which they committed depredations on travellers accompanied sometimes with the greatest cruelties. We dined at Jacquel, another town of the same character as Creal, the inn was dirty & miserable and poverty & filth was observable throughout the town. After dinner we ascended the mountains and found the road so stoney & rugged that we were obliged to get out of the carriage and walk tho the sun was exceeding hot. No houses were to be seen on these heights, but every thing shewed signs of sterility. In one place we pafsed a long tract of road that wound among rocks & precipices and where the frequent ascents & descents together with the badnefs of the road itself made it difficult for the carriage to get along. Here our Voiturier told us had been numerous robberies & murders committed, the robbers sometimes appearing in troops of twenty or thirty at a time and stripping the traveller of every thing, for the state of the road made it impofsible for either carriage or horseman to escape by flight.

The frequency of these depredations at length occasioned this road to be nearly deserted till the present excellent regulations of the police were carried into execution. Troops of Gens d'arms (soldiers in the service of the police) scoured the roads, ferreted out the robbers who were gullotined by dozens and put a complete stop to their enormities so that the road is as safe at present as any other in France and the people since they dear not *rob*, content themselves with *cheating* the travellers as much as pofsible.

In the evening we put up at Tourves a small town on the main road from Aix to Nice. Before we arrived at the town we pafsed the ruins of a magnificent chateau having charming pleasure grounds formerly belonging to a French Baron. He was gullotined in the revolution and his fine seat &c ruined. At supper, at the inn we had silver spoons with coats of arms engraved upon them, most probably the spoils of some chateau perhaps of the one above mentioned. This town, like most of the others in Provence, was extremely loathsome from the quantities of manure piled up against the houses which at certain seasons they carry into the fields & spread it about to fertilize the soil. The abominable smells occasioned by these heaps of manure, together with the vilenefs of the Inns destroy all idea of comfort to a traveller unaccustomed to them. Fortunately for me, my Canada jaunt of last summer had seasoned me in some measure for these disagreeables. When I enter one of these Inns where I am to pafs the night, I have but to draw a comparison between it and one of the log hovels into which we were huddled after a fatiguing days journey thro the wood and the inn appears a palace. For my part I try to take things as they come, with cheerfulnefs, and when I cannot get a dinner to suit my taste I endeavor to get a taste to suit my dinner. I have made a hearty meal of Cucumbers & onions off of a dirty table in a filthy log hut on the banks of Black river and I have made as hearty a one in a vile French auberge of a stale fowl that I verily believe had mounted guard on the table a half score of times. There is nothing I dread more than to be taken for one of the Smellfungii of this world. I therefore endeavor to be satisfied with the things round me when I find there is no use in complaining, and with the Master Mistrefs & servants of the inns when I perceive they have "all the dispositions in the world" to serve me. As Sterne says — "It is enough for

Heaven, and ought to be enough for me." I find indeed an advantage in this, I am attended with more cheerfulneſs & promptneſs than those who make the most complaints & curse the waiters.

[*September*] 11th

In the morning we sat out at day break and after riding sometime in a fog (the country being low & humid) we stopped to breakfast at Brignolles. At first they told us they had nothing to give us to eat but veal just killed, we made out however to get eggs, figs, grapes, cheese, bread wine &c and made a very comfortable meal.

The country began to grow much more fertile & picturesque. In one place I saw this years fourth crop of oats in great forwardneſs. Wine is very cheap from the numerous vineyards & abundant vintages. They sell last years wine in this part of the country for one *sous* a bottle exclusive of the bottle itself. The wine is harsh at first but in time becomes a very wholesaome pleasant table drink & has body sufficient to bear exportation to America. Grapes are 10 sous pr Cwt—between Vidauban & Fréjus, figs are sold 9 livres per cwt & 10 livres if they are packed up. People come here from Genoa & other places to purchase figs as these parts abound with them. In riding along, whenever we pleased we had at our command a fine regale of grapes & figs from the vineyards & plantations that were along the road. In the afternoon we paſsed by several places where they were gathering the Vintage. They do not celebrate it with that mirth and *gaieté de cœur* here as they do in other parts of France. The song, the dance, the inspiring sound of the pipe and tabor & the hospitable feast are the usual attendants of this happy season in some of the provinces "When Nature is pouring her abundance into everyone's lap and every eye is lifted up," "When Music beats time to *labor* and her children are rejoicing as they carry in their clusters." There it is really a "joyous riot of the affections," but here it is reduced to a level with the other rustic employments of plowing, threshing &c. In fact, the peasantry throughout the South of France have a stupidity & heavineſs of looks and manners that I had not expected to find among a people so celebrated for gaiety. For aught I know they may be very good hearted worthy people, for I could not understand their language sufficiently to talk with them. It is a barbarous jargon of French & Italian jumbled together in such a manner that neither French nor Italian can understand it without the greatest difficulty. A traveller is too apt to form his opinion of the lower claſs of people, from those that surround him, who are generally postillions, guides, servants, cicerones waiters &c &c the most mercenary wretches in existance. If you even make them a present for any little service they have rendered they will generally complain of the smallneſs of the gratuity, and I do not reccollect ever to have been thanked for money I gave in this manner *but once* and that was when for want of small change in my pocket I gave a fellow about six times as much as he deserved for showing me the inside of a church at Avignon.

I have had three or four sturdy fellows come lumbering up stairs to my chamber at a hotel with my portmanteau which all together did not weigh sixty weight, & every one of them demanded a recompense. I gave one of them who seemed to have sustained most of the weight a few sous and it was only by threatening to send for a *Gen d'Armes* that I got rid of the others.

In the evening we arrived at Vidauban and as the Inn seemed to have considerable company we took care to choose our rooms immediately.

[*September*] 12

We recommenced our route early in the morning and had a fatiguing hilly road to traverse. The country not very productive except in Figs which were in vast abundance. At half past ten we arrived at the small town of *Fréjus.* This town is pleasantly situated near the sea shore and was formerly a place of some trade and importance, it has declined into a state of poverty & insignificance. There are here a few Roman remains viz. An Ampitheatre, an Aqueduct which brought water from a neighboring hill—(only a few broken arches remaining) and some crumbling reliques of the Antient wall of the town. They are all in a very ruinous condition & are only worthy of curiosity from their antiquity. At this town Bonaparte & his suite landed on his return from Egypt. He debarked without performing Quarantine, a crime punishable with death according to the laws of the country which are very strict on vefsels from the Lavant. He did not remain longer in Fréjus than was sufficient to bring his things ashore & procure post horses & then sat off post haste for Paris—spreading astonishment by his unexpected appearance.

After dining at Fréjus we rode for some distance within sight of the Mediterranean and then began to ascend the Mountain of *Estrelles* one of the Maritime Alps said to be eight miles over. As the ascent in a little while became steep and laborious we got out and walked. The road wound up the Mountain in different directions, humoring the ascents and declivities, every now and then we caught a glimpse of the valley we had left—variegated with different plantations, vineyards &c bounded by the distant mountains on one side and on the other by the ocean calm and unruffled.

In one of the highest paſsages of the mountain we overtook two old women who solicited charity. They had been on a pilgrimage to a hermitage, among the mountains and were now returning to their native home near Milan in Italy. I was astonished to see two poor infirm old beings who seemed hardly able to support their own weight undertaking so long & toilsome [a] journey *on foot*. We could not understand them sufficiently to know the reason that induced them to make this pilgrimage.

The Sunset was rich & lovely. The highest points of the mountains were brightly illuminated while the lower ones were tinged with mellow colors and the distant valleys blended in the softest tones. The evening was calm & serene, the pure breeze of the mountains, loaded with perfumes from the Aromatic shrubs & herbs that grew on every side was refreshing and invigorating. The road had paſsed the highest eminence and after descending a little continued winding along the heights, often on the brink of vast precipices. At length about dusk we arrived at a house where the driver told us we must put up for the night as the next town was a considerable distance off and the road among the mountains too dangerous to think of paſsing it in the night. I did not at all like the looks of the house, it was large and solitary overhung by part of the mountain and embowered in thick trees, before the door some fellows were seated on a wooden bench drinking wine — they looked as rough as the mountains that surrounded us. On entering the Inn we desired the hostess to shew us to our rooms. She took a candle and we followed her up stairs to one end of the building where she opened the doors of two rooms in one of which were two and in the other three beds. The rooms would serve as perfect representations of the residence of poverty and Sloth. Dirty, without any furniture except one broken chair each, no glaſs in the windows, in short every thing had an appearance the most cheerleſs & forlorn — particularly to weary travellers who had need of comfortable accommodations to recover from their fatigue. We demanded of her to shew us her other rooms, she replied that these were all she had *furnished* and she was sure they were good enough. We were obliged therefore to be content and after a miserable supper we retired to one of the rooms the door of which we fastened as secure as poſsible. I confeſs I did not feel well at ease in this lodging. The wild and solitary situation of the house, the rough looks & manners of the people and their apparent indigence were sufficient to awaken disagreeable sensations, particularly as I knew this road had been much infested by robberies within the short space of 18 months or two years. In spight however of these uneasy reflections—of a hard bed and a host of hungry fleas I soon fell asleep and—this morning (13th) I had the pleasure of awaking (when the Voiturier knocked at the door) neither *robbd nor murdered.* We resumed our seats in the Voiture at daybreak today and pafsed thro a succefsion of wild & romantic mountain scenery with now and then a view of a distant valley all rendered more charming by the enlivening aid of a delightful morning. These mountains do not admit of cultivation in general—they are covered with Pines laurels box myrtle tamaric cyprefs &c & fragrant herbs & shrubs as Hyslop Thyme lavender &c. In some parts they afford subsistence to flocks of sheep that are driven upon them when the summer heats have scorched up the valleys, we observed flocks of them on some of the distant heights of an admirable whitenefs. At length we came again in sight of the Mediterranean and after long and rugged descents gained the valleys. After pafsing thro the little village of Cannes on the coast, we continued riding within a little distance of the shore having on the other side of us vineyards —figs & olives in luxurient plenty and behind them the Alps grandly terminating the prospect. These mountains as they approach the sea are by no means to be compared to those of the same chain in the interior (particularly in Savoy & Switzerland) either for height and singularity, they are by no means lofty enough to have snow on the top; but when I paſsed over them I fancied I could feel a considerable change in the atmosphere and that it was more pure & refreshing than in the valleys. We arrived at Antibes about mid day where we dined. This is a small seaport well fortified & garrisoned & formerly the frontier town of France. After leaving Antibes we paſsed thro S[t] Laurent, a small village where formerly they examined the trunks of travellers before they paſsed into Italy. There we croſsed the *Var* on a long wooden bridge. The river at this season is nearly dry. It was once the boundary between France & Italy. S[t] Laurent is said to be celebrated for its fine Muscadine wine.

In the evening we arrived at *Nice* and put up at the Hotel des Etrangers.

Nice 14th *Sept*[r]

Having thus happily accomplished my journey thro the *south of France* I felicitated myself with the idea that nothing farther was necefsary than to step into a Felluca & be wafted to the clafsic shore of Italy! I accordingly waited on the Municipality in company with the Doctor to deliver up my pafsport from Marseilles and obtain another one for Genoa. What was my surprize when the Secretary General having read my pafsport told me it was impofsible for him to grant me permifsion to depart. That I had come on with a pafsport such as is given to *suspected persons* and that I must remain here till a better pafsport came on, or an order from the Grand Judge *at Paris* authorizing my departure. This speech absolutely struck me dumb. The Doctor however, who spoke French far more fluently than I took up my cause and represented my situation, character, &c &c in as fair a light as pofsible, offered to pledge himself his property his all that I was veratibly an American Citizen and had demeaned myself peaceably & properly in France. In short he evinced the most friendly zeal and earnestnefs in my cause and said everything he could think of to induce the Secretary General to give me a pafsport.

The Secretary still made the same reply — it was out of his power — he was amenable to superior authority — or he would do it with the sincerest pleasure but that he would write to the Commifsary General of Police at Marseilles inclosing my pafsport and requesting another that would enable me to proceed.

He also afsured us that if I could procure a reclamation from any of our consuls he would forward me with pleasure the moment it arrived. In the meantime he gave me a letter of surety that should grant me the freedom of the town & protect me from molestation of police officers &c.

By the Doctor's advice I immediately wrote to Mr Schwartz & to our Consul Cathalin at Marseilles requesting them to represent my case to the Com: Genl: of their city & endeavor to have a good pafsport sent on immediately or if there was no other way—to reclaim me as an American citizen.

I have also written to a friend & to our Consul at Bordeaux requesting them to take the same measures there. Dr Henry leaves this place in a day or two and has promised to use his exertions to have me reclaimed at Genoa. I have written by him to my friend S—— at the latter place and do not doubt but he will exert his friendship to the utmost so that it will be hard if I do not receive relief from one quarter or another.

[*September*] 15th

Feeling indisposed after dinner this afternoon I went to my chamber, laid down & soon fell asleep.

I was suddenly awakened by the noise of some persons entering the room, & found before me an officer of the Police and the Doctor. The former had come to demand my papers to carry before the mayor for some particular reasons. The Dr told me not to disturb myself—that he would accompany the man & learn what was the occasion of this visit. In about half an hours time I heard the Doctor coming up stairs humming a tune in a hideous manner in a tone of voice like that of Tom Pipes between a *screech & a whistle*. He entered my room with a furious countenance and throwing himself into a chair, stopped in the middle of his tune & began to curse the police in a most voluble manner nor could I get a word from him till he had consigned every mothers son of them to the infernal regions.

He then let me know that I had been denounced by some scoundrel of a Spy, for an *Englishman* which had occasioned the demand for my papers. He had seen the adjoinat of the Mayor who spoke English & was very polite; by his representations he had prepofsefsed him in my favor.

I changed my drefs & accompanied the Doctor before the adjoinat, who gave me a very civil reception, told me he was sensible of the folly of the suspicions that had been indulged against me, and afsured me that my tranquility should not again be disturbed while I remained in Nice. Having received my papers from him we returned to the Hotel.

[*September*] 17th

This morning the Doctor sat sail in a Felucca for Genoa and tho I could not but feel regret at parting with a man whose company was so agreeable & who had proved himself so much my friend yet I was satisfied on one Account as it would facilitate my own departure for I look chiefly to Genoa for effectual afsistance. As I did not expect to make any stay at Nice I brought on but one letter of introduction, to Mr Guide [?] one of the principal merchants of the place. Like most French merchants, however, he is too much wrapped up in Commercial affairs & too intent on making money to pay much attentions to a stranger from whom he cannot expect *profitable returns.* I make out, however, to pafs away the time pretty tolerably by writing, reading walking &c. The Maitre de hotel where I reside is a Swifs, with all the honesty & goodnefs of heart that characterizes his nation. He spares no pains to render my situation agreeable & whenever I walk into the country one of his sons is sent with me as a guide, to shew me the gardens &c. I cannot but laugh at the blackguardism of the common soldiery with which I am greeted sometimes as I walk the streets. They mistake me for an Englishman—indeed half the people in France that are not well informed hardly know but that America appertains to England and that we are in the same situation in regard to them as Scotland or Ireland. Others again place us in quite another quarter of the globe. I was asked the other day at dinner by a well drefsed Frenchman whether my *province* (for he took the United States to be a mere province) was not a great wine country and whether it was not in the neighborhood of *Turkey* or *somewhere there about!* Another time I was accosted by a French officer "Vous êtes Anglais monsieur" said he—"Pardonnez moi" replied I "Je suis des Etats Unis d'Amérique"—"Eh bien—c'est la même chose"!

[*September*] 24th

Yesterday was the thirteenth anniversary of the French republic and the commencement of a New Year according to their present Calendar. It was necefsary therefore to celebrate it with some rejoicing as we do the fourth of July in America. These national fêtes are seldom kept up with vigor for any length of time among this fickle people. They now wait for a *new batch* of public days, such as the birth day of the Emperor — the anniversary of the Coronation &c. But in the present instance as the fête was not absolutely abolished it was requisite *for decencys sake* to make some shew of rejoicing. There was therefore some firing of cannon — some shutting of shops & some shew of holliday approns. In the Evening the house of the Municipality was superbly illuminated with a couple of paper lanthorns in each window and one of the public walks was brilliantly lighted up by ½ a dozen tar buckets & pots of turpentine elevated on posts at certain distances by the light of which the soldiery & lower people amused themselves with dancing.

The day paſsed off with decency and decorum nor did I observe any of that amusement going forward so fashionable among our *Mobility* of boxing & cudgeling. The quarrels among the lower claſs in this country are generally settled by the *tongue* and he that has the most volubility & strongest lungs carries the day.

I never saw a contest of fisty cuffs in France but once, and that was between two Porters in Bordeaux & they managed it in so clumsy a manner that it was evident they were but novices in the busineſs. Three or four Americans had stopped to enjoy the *fun* but they soon got out of patience on the combattants kicking scratching pulling hair &c —

and went off damning them for brutes that did not know how to box *like men.*

You may wish to know something of Nice, where I am vegetating so very agreeably. It is charmingly situated in a small valley bounded on one side by the Sea and on the other by an Ampitheatre of Hills which rise gradually and are covered to the top with gardens vineyards, olive, orange, lemon, pomgranate trees &c & diversified by handsome white country seats. Behind these hills the Alps rise in more lofty and majestic heights. The highly cultivated state of the valley and hills gives the prospect a luxurient verdure. As most of the trees are evergreens they retain this appearance all the year. Properly speaking there is no winter here as the climate is so mild that the fruits and flowers flourish equally well in that season as in the others. It is delightful to walk out into the Country and visit the Gardens; the Oranges & lemons are not yet ripe but there is abundance of Grapes figs pomegranates &c. Nice is but a small place containing about ten or twelve thousand inhabitants. The houses are neat, built of stone and painted very ingeniously in imitation of stucco work arround the doors & windows — a manner customary in the Italian towns.

The streets are very narrow and dirty except in the west end of the town (where I reside) where the houses are well built—generally four Stories high & uniform. There is a pleasant walk along the sea shore on a terrace built on the roofs of a range of small houses—caffés &c, it is paved with small stones over which is laid a thick coat of excellent plaister or cement so that it is very even & agreeable to the feet. The country also, in the vicinity of the town affords delightful promenades. The weather is very warm at present but the mornings and evenings are cool & bracing. Musquitos gnats &c are very troublesome here, but Musquito curtains are universally used for the beds, which prevents their tormenting at night. The chief employments of the inhabitants are making oil wine & cordage. The privateers that infest the coasts have injured very much the Commerce of Nice. The common people speak *the Patois* (a Jargon of French & Italian) in the highest degree corrupt so that it is impossible for me to understand them. Nice is defended by some small batteries of Cannon and a fort on Monte Albano, a high rocky bluff which terminates the City on the east & runs into the sea.

The port is defended by a mole and does not appear capable of receiving very large vessels. The vessels that I saw in the port were generally Feluccas & such small craft & one little Brig. At the back of the town runs the river Paglion & empties itself into the sea west of the town. At present it is almost dry but in rainy seasons—spring time &c it is filld by the snows & floods from the mountains. In this part of the country they raise a great deal of hemp some rice barley wheat &c & Indian corn (the latter is raised in great quantities in Languedoc—along the Garonne &c. Neither the stalk nor ears are by any means as large as in America).

The winds are very variable here and in Summer there is often much ficklenefs in the climate which occasions colds pluresies fevers rheumatism &c. In the Spring the winds are very keen from pafsing over the Alps which are then covered with snow. The people of Nice are said to be subject to Scrophulas rheumatisms scorbutic complaints &c. The Winters are very mild and peculiarly agreeable to persons suffering under pulmonary complaints. The falls are wet. The climate bad for scorbutic habits. Nice formerly was an Italian town & situated in Piedmont—at present it appertains to France, has a French garrison & is the chief place (*chef lieu*) of the department of the Alpes Maritimes. In time of peace vast numbers of English invalids resort here to pafs the winter which makes it lively & fashionable. At present it is dull & stupid, the only public amusement being a wretchedly performed play in a miserable theatre twice or three times a week. A French garrison by no means enlivens a place as the officers seem to have but little of that gallantry and spirit of polite amusement that is necefsary to promote public diversions &c.

The Accounts I read in the Paris papers of the yellow fever's having made its appearance in New York is by no means calculated to raise my spirits which are deprefsd by lonesomenefs & chagrin. I have not the hopes of hearing from you or any of my friends while here, as my letters are directed to be forwarded to Italy, this adds to my impatience to get on.

[*September*] 26th

I have just received two or three letters and I cannot exprefs the agreeable revolution they have occasioned in my feelings. They were put into my hands by my landlord just as I returned from one of my solitary morning rambles along the sea shore, where I had been contemplating the ocean & wishing myself on its bosom in full sail to Genoa. The first packet was from my indefatigable friend Dr Henry inclosing a letter from T H S—— and a reclamation from our consul, all obtained & dispatched in lefs than twenty four hours after his arrival. As to the letter from S—— it breathes all the warmth of heart & openeſs of soul that distinguishes that worthy fellow. He expreſses his delight & surprize at finding me so near him, his sorrow at my embarraſsments & regret that his situation will not allow him to haste here & meet me. He urges me to make no delay in coming to him "My dear fellow" says he "you know the offer of my *Uncle Toby* to poor *sick Lefevre*—with the same honesty of soul I tender the same in *every respect* to you." I do not know how to expreſs the delightful emotions this letter has occasioned. To meet an old friend so far from home—*and such a friend* too—Heavens—it is an extacy I have been anticipating in all my journyings in France. Dr Henry speaks highly in his letter of S——'s hospitable and friendly reception of him in consequence of an introductory letter from me—and of the zeal S—— displayed in dispatching my busineſs. In consequence of their united exertions certificates &c a reclamation was immediately procured & as promptly forwarded.

I have also received a pacquet from our Consul Mr Cathalin at Marseilles representing my case to the Préfet of Nice & urging him to give me a paſsport for Italy. Thus is my situation happily releived and I have but to get a paſsport & then away for Italy & S——

Evening

"Ye Gods: If theres a man I ought to hate
"Attendance & dependance be his fate!"

I never felt the force of these lines of Swift more than I have today when I have been dancing attendance on Mr Le Sécrétaire Général from morning till night without being able to see him. At last I had to give the reclamation & letter to one of the head clerks to carry them to the préfet or Sec Gen: After waiting some time in sanguine hopes, or rather in certainty of a paſsport being ordered me the clerk returned with the pleasing intelligence that I must wait "*quelques jours*" (some days) till an answer was received to a letter that had been written to the Commiſsary General at Marseilles. What this letter is about or why I have to wait for it I cannot conceive, surely the reclamation of our Consul is sufficient. I never wanted a knowledge of the language so much as when the clerk brought this answer. I fairly gasped for words. As it was, I gave him my sentiments pretty roundly in the best French I could utter. The Secretary had promised that when a reclamation was presented from our Consul I should be forwarded with pleasure and now that it is obtained supported by a letter from our Consul at Marseilles I am still detained. I am apprehensive they intend to keep me here till the decision of the

Grand Judge at Paris is obtained conformable to the words of my paſsport. If so, I cannot tell how much longer I may be obliged to rest here. This it is to have to deal with *Dogs in office*, however I am in their power and *patience par force* must be my motto.

[*September*] 29th

I called the day before yesterday in the morning on Monsieur G——, a French merchant of this place to whom I had brought a letter of introduction and mentioned to him my situation. He desired me to leave my reclamation &c with him and he would visit the Préfet with whom he was acquainted—and represent my case to him. I called on him today and he told me he had seen Mr De Buty the Secretary particulier and that the answer still was that it was not in their power to give me a paſsport, that they would write immediately to Marseilles for the paſs-port with which I came on to Marseilles from Bor-deaux—and when they received it they would send it on to Paris to the Grand Judge, and on his de-cision being sent in my favor they would give me a paſsport to proceed *with pleasure*. Thus have I the agreeable prospect of waiting here near a Month nor do I know even if I will obtain a paſsport then. I have been so repeatedly amused and bantered here with promises and false accounts that my confidence in their veracity is entirely destroyed.

*Oct*r 5th

NOTHING has since occurred to alter my situation. The weather has been unsettled & rainy. This morning however was clear & beautiful & I set off very early to visit Villefranche a small town about a league & a half from Nice on the sea shore. We ascended the mountains to the east of the city and after a rugged ascent which however was rendered lefs fatigueing from the variety of picturesque prospects with which it was enlivened we at length arrived at an Emenence that commanded a charming & extensive view. The Sides of the mountain were as a continued Garden, embellished with white country seats &c & they gradually swept down into the beautiful & luxuriently cultivated valley of Nice. The town lay at a distance below us, its spires gilded by the first rays of the sun, beyond it spread the unruffled Medditerranean speckled here and there with the bark of a fisherman.

The Ampitheatre of hills that surround the valley seemed from the height from which we viewd them to be almost level & like the valley presented to the eye the rich & refreshing verdure of Oranges citrons Olives & vineyards. Behind them the Alps reared their rocky summits and gradually melted into distance. In the *foreground* of the picture the Mountain ascended to a height steep & rugged called Monte Albano on which is seated the Castle of Nice.

While we were enjoying the prospect we were overtaken by two Polonese noblemen whom I had formed an acquaintance with in Nice and who were going by land on mules to Genoa.

After proceeding together for some time we came to where the road parted, when I took leave of them but I could perceive them now & then for a long time as their road wound among the heights. We afterwards descended to Villefranche which is very romantically situated in a small hollow at the foot of the mountains & partly built on the ascent of one of them. Here is a Chateau in which the criminals vagabonds &c of Nice are confined. There is also a good & deep port defended by a mole. On a point that runs out into the sea to the east of Villefranche is the *Fanale* or light house of Nice. From Villefranche we returned by water in a small boat to Nice and the pleasantneſs of the weather made the sail delightful.

[*October*] 8th

I received a letter from Wm Lee Esqr our Consul at Bordeaux in reply to one I wrote him the 15th of September. He mentions that he had applied to the Commifsary General of Police to rectify my pafsport but had not yet received an answer. He had also written to our minister at Paris requesting him to interest himself in my favor.

[*October*] 9th

I took a walk into the country in company with two young physicians one Italian the other French, to examine some Roman ruins situated among the mountains at some distance from the town. The ruins consisted of an Ampitheatre and a temple of Diana. Of the former some arcades remained in a crumbling condition but the space of the Arena was still distinct & was converted into a little plantation of olive trees which seemed to say that the bloody scenes & contentions that had once reigned there, had given place to peace & tranquility. The temple of Diana has been converted into an habitation for Peasants so that its genuine appearance is much altered. Both buildings are constructed with small square stones with layers of thin broad bricks at certain intervals like the ampitheatre at Bordeaux. This has been the Scite of some Roman town but from the smallnefs of the ampitheatre it could not have been very considerable.

[*October*] 14th

I have received a very polite letter from Robt L Livingston Esqr Son in law of the Minister mentioning that a letter has been received by the Minister from Mr Lee of Bordx and that they had also received sometime since some letters that I had sent on from Bordeaux written by the Mrs [*Minister's*] friends in America which mentioned me particularly. That therefore as soon as the Minister had heard of my embarrafsments he sent a pafsport immediately to the Grand Judge for his signature and that it would most probably come on by that or the next boat. Two carriers however have arrived without the pafsport.

This morning I went to the Cathederal to see grand mafs performed in presence of the Préfet & other authorities & the soldiers of the Garrison.

The Cathederal is handsomely decorated in the interior but the paintings of value have been removed and inferior ones substituted. The music of the regiment played at different times during the service. At a signal given by the drum all the soldiers — (who were in the middle of the church) presented arms knelt down and were *supposed* to pray for the space of a moment when at another signal they rose up & shouldered their muskets. This may have a good effect in habituating the soldiery to have a respect for religion, but it is somewhat whimsical to see *praying* introduced into the manual exercise. In the evening, I received a visit from Mr Lowel an American Gentleman who arrived last evening on his route to Italy. I accompanied him to his lodgings and was introduced to his wife and sister. The sight of some Americans in this corner of France was cheering & reviving and I experienced the truth of the poets words

"*How with a brothers look a brothers smile*
The stranger greets each native of his isle."

[*October*] 17th

After five weeks detention wherein I had been continuously baffled disappointed and abused with false promises I at length was relieved by the pafsport from Mr Livingston who has behaved to me in a very handsome manner. After arranging matters with the police I sat sail this morning in a Felucca for Genoa. There were seven [of] us from the *Hotel des Etrangers* all French officers excepting a young German who talks English perfectly and myself. In the felucca we found three other officers. They were going to join their regiment which is stationed in the Genoese territories.

The weather was delightful and the sea calm as

the Mediterranean most generally is. We coasted along partly sailing & partly rowed always keeping near the shore for fear of the little privateers that infest the coast (These privateers are termed always *English* tho very often there is but one Englishman aboard & the rest of the crew are made up of Genoese Maltese Spaniards &c. They are very unprincipled and are in fact complete pirates).

The shore was a continual succefsion of Mountains rocky & barren yet the lower parts cultivated with great industry so as to resemble a perfect forest of olives, oranges, citrons &c.

The mountains were skirted with villages towns, &c which had a most picturesque appearance from the water some of them being perched on the point of precipices that seemed rather as the haunts of eagles than of men.

As there was a little swell in the sea my fellow pafsengers soon became sea sick and cascaded most violently. Three or four of the officers had never been on the sea before and made such hideous contortions of the features that I could not but laugh. One of them eyed me askance with a rueful exprefsion of countenance and said I might laugh if I pleased — but that he should certainly die before we arrived at Genoa. I told him not to be cast down, & drawing a roasted leg of fat mutton out of my provision basket, I asked him if he would not take a slice by way of medicine. The sight of the mutton sent the poor devil to the side of the veſsel in a moment and acted like a powerful emetic. One of the officers had been in the French navy and was ashamed to be sea sick. I could perceive however that there was an insurrection in his bowels — he turned as pale as a ghost but still continued to keep his stomach within proper bounds till a sudden pitch of the veſsel overcame all his precautions & he continued vomiting for an half hour. He would not however alow he was sea sick but laid it all to the account of the breakfast he had eaten and between every strain would exclaim "Ah le villain chocolat!"

We paſsed the town of Monaco formerly the capital of a small principality of that name. It contains about nine hundred persons and is situated on a flat rock that runs into the sea having a very picturesque appearance. We also paſsed Vingtimiglia where the Genoese territories commence — Bordighera &c & several Villages of small importance but very prettily situated in well cultivated spots at the foot of the mountains. Towards sun down we arrived at St Remo a town built on the slope of a hill and making a very handsome appearance from the water. As our party was rather large (consisting of ten) we had a difficulty in finding accommodations. There were but two hotels in the place the *Post* & the *Marine hotel* and as the former was the best we went there. The Landlord told us he had but one vacant bed in the house, that a number of French troops had filled the town on their way to Genoa. The man I believe was afraid the officers intended to be billeted upon him and he knew they were rather unprofitable lodgers. As soon however as they aſsured him they meant to pay the same as other travellers he reccollected three or four beds were unoccupied. We therefore made out to find lodgings the officers sleeping two in a bed and a mattraſs being given to me—two or three of the officers slept at the Marine hotel where they were entertained by a host of fleas. Our own hotel did not afford much matter of congratulation. It was dark and dirty and miserably off for attendance. As soon as we had settled our arrangements for the night and ordered supper I took a walk to see the town in company with the young German and one of the officers. In the lower part of the town the streets were narrow but clean but as we ascended they became extremely small dark and intricate winding about in a singular manner and often for considerable distances having the houses built over them so that they appeared to be vaulted subterraneous pafsages. The sun never penetrated into these dark places and many of them hardly would admit a feeble twilight. They were so steep that even mules themselves seemed hardly able to travel them. After attaining the summit of the hill we arrived in front of a handsome building but whether convent or seminary I could not learn. From hence there is a very fine view of the surrounding country, the hills covered with vines olives oranges pomegranates &c and interspersed with pretty white country seats. The town swept down from the plain where we stood to the ocean and as the weather was clear we could perceive the highlands of Corsica at a great distance. The town of St Remo is well peopled. There are two or three convents for men & women & several churches. I could immediately perceive that I had left the French dominions from the situation of the latter—unplundered and the statues pictures &c undefaced by the fury of revolutionary mobs.

[*October*] 18th

Early in the morning we again set sail with a light breeze and delightful weather. We glided pleasantly past the villages of Larma Santa la Riva St Stephano (or St Lorenzo) and came in sight of the flourishing town of Port Mauritio (or Port Maurice). The wind had by this time come ahead and blew rather strong, however we might very easily have beat in to Porto Mauritio but one of the officers was frightened and prevailed upon the Padrone to put back for St Stephano. There the surf ran so high that we dared not approach the shore but had to cast anchor & get the people of the village to come off to us with a large fishing boat. This they did very cheerfully and when they arrived where the surf broke they jumped into the water & carried us on their back to land. After this they labored for near an hour in dragging our felucca ashore on the sands as they feared a strong gale of wind. In reward for their goodneſs and the trouble & fatigue they had undergone laboring so long in the water I proposed that we should each give them something. This the officers did not appear to relish, and two or three of them strongly opposed it. I was surprized at such meaneſs so incompatable with the character of soldiers but before we arrived at Genoa I saw several more instances which seemed to corroborate the reputation the French Soldiery have, of being very penurious & niggardly. The young German had seconded me very warmly in the proposal & at last to induce the others to join he mentioned the small sum of *twenty sous* about 18 cents. Still however they declined till I declared I would pay for all of them myself rather than the poor people should go unrewarded. This piqued their pride and they reluctantly paid the money. As there was no prospect of being able to resume our voyage that day and the village did not offer even tolerable accommodations we determined to walk to Porto Mauritio about three leagues distant and wait there the arrival of our felucca. We therefore engaged two boys to carry our night bags and sat out in the heat of the day. The road is the high way from Nice to Genoa along the sea and is only practicable for mules & afses and indeed I hardly see how they get along it. It is very stoney & rugged cut along the face of the mountains sometimes ascending like stairs scarcely wide enough for two animals to pafs & nothing to secure them in case of a stumble from falling down the precipices into the sea. Those sure footed animals, notwithstanding, traverse them with perfect safety with enormous loads—indeed it is generally observed that mules will pafs where men dare not trust themselves. The sun was powerful and the reflection from the face of the mountain rendered it almost insupportable. To add to our vexations the wind sprung up favorably by the time we had accomplished half of our walk & we had the mortification to see that if we had not have turned back from Porto Mauritio we might have made several more leagues this day.

Porto Mauritio is built on a rocky hill and from the sea makes a handsome shew. Our auberge was below the town on the shore and we were too fatigued to walk up and examine the place. This town & Oneglia another little place about a mile & half distant furnish oil which is said to be the best of the whole Riviera. They have much demand for it. When I arrived at the auberge I found the boy who had carried a small packet for me and a large night bag for one of the officers bitterly complaining. He had carried the things on his head in the heat of the sun for six miles and in reccompence the officer had given him 10 sous (about eight or nine cents). I could not but exprefs my contempt of such meannefs and gave the boy a reward with which he seemed highly delighted. The officer observed that "*Les Mefsieurs anglaises* were always more rich than wise—that it was not in every ones power to pay equally well." I replied that "I never demanded the labor of other people unlefs I intended to pay them justly for it and that whenever I could not afford to hire the services of others I always served myself."

I was disgusted at the mean spirit of those officers. They cavild with every innkeeper about his prices tho I was convinced the poor devil charged them at the lowest rates, and they invariably gave the servants nothing but curses for their pains. Our Lodgings at Porto Mauritio were miserable and the supper ill cooked and served up in a most slovenly manner.

[*October*] 19th

Our veſsel having arrived over night we set sail this morning at an early hour and continued coasting along within our usual distance from the shore continually amused with the variety of prospect and the continual succeſsion of towns villages convents, chateaus &c that skirted the mountains & crowned the inferior hills. This chain of mountains that form the Genoese coast is a part of the Grand chain of Appenines that run thro Italy and connect with the Alps.

In the middle of the day we paſsed by the little town of Albenga opposite which stands a small rocky island of the same name on which a vast number of rabbits are said to exist. The country about Albenga produces considerable quantities of hemp.

Just before we paſsed this Island a shot was fired ahead of us by a small felucca privateer in shore who suspected from the number of us on board that we were one of the little privateers that infest the coast. Our Padrone immediately displayed the Genoese flag & haild the privateer. Either they did not see & hear him or their suspicions were very strong for they fired another shot at us which whistled just over our heads. Three or four of the officers immediately popped into the small hold of the felucca & crammed themselves among the trunks. The Padrone waved his flag & bawled repeatedly with all his might & they suffered us to paſs without further molestation. In the afternoon at 5 oclock we arrived opposite Noli where the Padrone would have put in but we insisted upon his continuing on to Savona about 3 or 4 leagues further on, he consented tho very unwillingly. Cape Noli is a remarkable bluff that rises perpendicular out of the sea to a considerable height & is very difficult to paſs when the weather is stormy. The waves have formed caverns in various places and the breakers dashing into them when the wind is high make a noise that is awful even to the felucca men who are in some degree habituated to them.

Some time ago the people of a privateer ascended one of the heights of this cape to look out if there were any veſsels in sight when they discovered a cavern in the rock with implements for coining &c. This had been the working place of a Gang of Coiners who had drove their trade most spiritedly some years ago. Rewards had been offered by the state for their apprehension & numerous attempts had been made to find out their retreat but all in vain. They had made their fortunes & abandoned their hiding place which was thus accidentally discovered. The coiners have left a monument of industry behind them as it must have required infinite labor & patience to make an aperture thro the rock in one place to admit light into their cavern. The town of Noli & the surrounding parts afford fine subjects for the landscape painter being charmingly picturesque.

The breeze which sprung up opposite Noli soon died away and the men had to take to the oars. The evening that succeeded was calm & serene and by the aid of a bright moonlight we could distinguish the white villages churches &c. And now and then the Vesper bell of some convent situated among the mountains would seem to linger over the calm surface of the sea and to be in perfect unison with the scene. The men belonging to the felucca were all Genoese & shewed a degree of religious respect that I had lookd in vain for in France. When they heard the bell sound for vespers they stopped rowing pulled off their caps made the sign of the crofs & repeated their *Ave Maria*. About half past seven or eight oclock we arrived at Savona, a large town, the port of which is defended by a Mole & capable of receiving large ships tho I saw nothing there but small craft. Here is an excellent college for the education of youth.

When we entered the port we found everything silent & on hailing the shore we were informed that the Gates were shut & that we could not be admitted. We now began to wish we had not forced the padrone to continue on to this place—a northerly wind had sprung up which made it quite cold and as we had eat nothing since the morning but dry bread we began to feel quite hungry. Luckily one of the officers was a French Commifsary—he demanded to be landed mentioned his rank &c &c and after much dispute and nearly an hours shivering in the cold we were permitted to land.

Here the same difficulty of finding accommodations occurred that we had experienced the whole voyage and I was content to pafs the night on a straw bed on which however I slept most soundly.

[*October*] 20

We parted from Savona by daylight. The city made a beautiful appearance when viewd from the entrance of the harbor and is certainly charmingly situated. We had Genoa now full in view and were in high spirits at the prospects of a speedy arrival.

The shore presented a continual string of villages very close to each other. Albisolla which contains a magnificent palace—Novi—Voltri, *Sestri di Ponente* &c and among others the small village of Cocorato famous for being the birthplace of Christopher Columbus. It is about [*blank*] leagues from Genoa [situated] pleasantly on the shore with the mountains gradually rising behind it. After having sailed past several villages in the vicinity of Genoa & adorned with the Villas of the Genoese Nobility we at length paſsed the magnificent suburbs called St Pietra d'Arena & entered the harbor of Genoa about one oclock. The city had a Striking appearance to me when I entered between the Moles that guard the harbor and saw the town like an ampitheatre around it. The houses rise one above another in consequence of the hills on which they are built, so that the town shews to a vast advantage & cannot but strike the most indifferent observer. After stopping at the health office & displaying our bills of health we landed at a fine Stone Quay and were immediately surrounded by a herd of Porters beggars & Vagabonds. Three or four laid hold of my trunk and as I did not speak their language they pretended not to know what I meant when I ordered them to put it down till I collared one of the fellows and one of my fellow paſsengers interfered & delivered it into the hands of a public Porter. We were stopped at the gate by a custom house officer who had his little office just by and said our trunks must be examined. I was in company with one of the officers who told the custom house officer that we were French officers and had no need to have our trunks searchd. The man then hinted that if we would give him *something* he would wave the ceremony. With this I was going to comply when my companion swore I should not, that I was one of the Emperors soldiers and they had no right to demand it.

For my part I said nothing as my English accent would soon have given the lie to his afsertion, but I could not but laugh heartily. We were therefore suffered to pafs with a few curses from the custom house officer.

The best hotel in Genoa is the *Hotel de Ville* or rather it is the most fashionable. I was reccomended to the *Hotel di Torri* which I believe is nearly as good at least I was so well satisfied with it that I never thought it worth while to change my lodgings. As soon as I had changed my clothes at the Hotel I called upon S—— and received a welcome the most open and friendly imaginable. It is impofsible to exprefs the rapture I felt at meeting with a particular friend so far from home and after having been so long among strangers.

[*October*] 25th

Genoa is the capital of the Ligurian or Genoese Ripublick (antiently called Genua capital of the Ligurian tribes in the time of the Roman republick). It is as I before observed, situated on the side of a hill making a semicircle round the harbor, from whence the best view of it is to be obtained. It is computed to contain about [*blank*] inhabitants. This city is celebrated for the magnificence of the palaces which have obtained for it the title of *Genoa the Superb*. The finest of those palaces are situated in the two principal streets the *Strada Nuova* and *Strada Balbi*. These present a continued string of grand buildings on each side of the way — decorated with marbles and some of them painted in fresco on the exterior walls with histories of Battles &c. Those streets are termed by the English the *Streets of Palaces*, and it is said that all Europe cannot furnish streets with such a continued succefsion of magnificent architecture. The narrownefs of the streets however prevent the palaces from being seen to advantage for tho they are the two widest in the city, yet in general they are not above thirty feet wide. As to the other streets of Genoa — they hardly deserve the names of alleys some of them being but six seven & eight feet wide and I have been obliged to turn back or get into the door of a house to make way for an Afs with a pannier on each side that was walking in the middle of the street. The streets are well paved and generally very clean.

The city is surrounded by two walls one of which is built round the town itself and the other takes in all the commanding heights. There is a charming ride on horseback on the outer wall as you have prospects of Genoa the harbor & the surrounding country from different points of View.

The churches are very rich in marbles fresco & oil paintings, carvings &c. The walls are coverd with Scripture pieces in frescos.

In the church of St Ambrogio are three very fine oil paintings viz. the *Circumcision* by Rubens over the high altar. 2^d^ *St Ignatius exorcising a demoniac & raising dead children to life* by the same painter but placed in so dark a chaple that the figures cannot be seen except the heads where the lights of the picture are most strongly thrown. 3^d^ The *Assumption of the Virgin* a most charming piece by Guido.

The Cathederal dedicated to St Laurence is of a Gothic construction. This saint sufferd martyrdom in Rome in the year 280 and they immediately converted the house where he lodged in Genoa on his way from Spain to Rome into a church. In 985 it was made the cathedral but still bears the name of the saint. Over the Grand entrance is a carved figure of the Saint broiling on a gridiron (the manner of his death) and two grotesque looking figures blowing up the fire with small bellows's. The church is incrusted both the inside & the exterior with black & white marble & paved with the same.

The chief treasures of this church were said to be the bones of St John the Babtist preserved in the chapel of the same name and an Emerald dish which was the Genoese share of the plunder of Cesarea when that city was captured by the Crusaders, others say it was presented by Baldwin King of Jerusalem. It has been pretended by some to have been the same dish out of which our Saviour eat at the last supper, (tho if I reccollect right the supper was eaten at an Inn where it is not likely they would serve their Guests in Emerald dishes). Lastly some affirm that the dish was one of the presents made by Queen Sheba to Solomon. Whoever gave the dish or however great its antiquity it must certainly be a precious article for it is said to be 14½ inches in diameter. For my part I did not see either the Bones of St John or the Dish of King Solomon for I forgot to enquire for either. The walls of the Cathederal were formerly painted in fresco but they have lately been white washed in a desperate fit of cleanlineſs.

The church of the *Annonciata* is in the square of the same name and is one of the Richest churches of Genoa in marbles & workmanship. It is built at the Expence of the Lomellino family by two brothers of that name. They are said to have differd about the manner in which they should finish the front of the church which has therefore never been compleated.

Over the grand entrance in the interior is a large painting of the last supper by Julius Caesar Procaccini which is very much admired. It is not in a good light and the picture is much darkend by time. It is counted one of the Chef d'ouvres of that painter.

St Maria di Carignano has two or three good paintings by Procaccini. There are two statues by Puget the famous French Sculptor. One of them — St Sebastiano — is a representation of that martyr bound to a tree & half flead alive, and pofsefses great merit as does the other which is St Allefsandro Pauli. In front of this church is the remarkable bridge of Carignano that joins the hill of the same name to that of Sarzano. It has four arches is 90 feet high 45 wide & 160 or 170 paces long — from the top of it you see houses & streets below you. The armory that formerly contained (besides a vast number of stands of arms) — several suits of antient armor & antient implements of war was plunderd by the French when they took poſseſsion of Genoa. Some of the mob ran about the streets with helmets on their heads. Two or three of the helmets have been hoisted on liberty poles & transformed to liberty caps and many of them were converted by taylors into chafing dishes to heat their irons on — In which humble occupation I saw many of them employed in different parts of Genoa. Several of the Suits of Armor are hung up in the entrance to the court yard of the Doges palace.

I visited yesterday the palace of the great Andrea Doria. This is one of the most antient of Genoa and was formerly of great Splendor. It is at present deserted & neglected, its poſseſsors residing in palaces leſs capacious & uncomfortable. The long suites of Splendid appartments stripped of their furniture—the rich tapestry faded & torn, had a dreary & melancholy appearance. These are the chief of the churches & palaces I have yet seen tho there are others in Genoa well worthy of attention.

The Theatre is a mean looking building on the outside and the interior is very ill contrived. It is very large and high a circumstance extremely unfavorable to the voices of the actors. There are about two hundred boxes which are all hired by the year. Those who have no box seat themselves in that part of the theatre which we call the pit, which has a number of rows of benches with backs to them. The same ticket that admits you here admits you likewise to any other part of the house and you pay about 20 Sous for it. The Boxes are partitioned off from each other and only open in front where they generally have curtains by which means they can entirely seclude themselves from the audience. They are likewise furnished with sofas, chairs, tables &c and in carnival time it is very common to sup, play at cards &c in the boxes. The stage only is illuminated as the ladies complain that lights placed in the other part of the theatre *hurt their eyes!* Besides they say if the theatre was illuminated they would have to take pains in drefsing themselves whereas at present they can go to the theatre in an undrefs.

Indeed an Italian theatre is the most accommodating public place imaginable. The scenery is pretty good. My ignorance of the language renderd it impossible for me to judge of the dialogue but the music was very fine. All the Operas at present exhibited in Genoa are Buffa (or comic). They in a manner chant all the dialogue which has a singular & unnatural appearance to a stranger. The chief drollery of the piece seemd to lie in the grimaces & whimsical faces & attitudes of one of the performers who exerted his talent in this respect to a most extravagant and unnatural degree yet in spight of the contempt I felt for such buffoonery I could not but laugh at some of his distortions of countenance & figure.

It is forbidden here for the audience to *encore* and I highly approve of the regulation. When any Actor sings a song well, or performs a scene with skill — on his exit the audience continue clapping till he reappears and bows an acknowledgement of their applause.

This is so frequently done in the course of a play that it becomes fatiguing to one not accustomed to it. At the benefit of a performer the theatre is illuminated very brilliantly and a person (sometimes the actor) stands near the entrance or sits at a table placed there, with a box to receive the donations of those who enter. The admirers of the performer very often make handsome presents; and without this the benefit would be very inconsiderable, from the low price of the tickets.

The Genoese women are generally well made with handsome features and very fine black eyes. They are infinitely superior in my opinion to the French women in respect to personal charms.

They are much given to intrigue, exceeding amorous and in case of neglect it is said revengeful. As to the latter however it is not so much the case at present as it was formerly. The Stilleto is forbidden to be worn and Genoa that was once one of the worst places in Italy for afsafsinations no longer deserves the character.

In this respect a change has taken place all over Italy and the French I believe deserve a great part of the merit of effecting it. The Afsafsinations now are very rare and generally take place among the lower clafs in their quarrels.

[*October*] 26th

Yesterday morning made an excursion into the country to visit Sestri a small village about six miles to the west of Genoa. I was in company with Storm and Mr Cafferana an English gentleman; we intended to visit the Lomellino Gardens near Sestri, which are laid out in the English taste and much admired. Our road lay along the shore of the Medditeranean and as we rode along we were presented with a variety of charming prospects. We passd thro the suburbs of St Pietra d' Arena in which are some fine palaces tho much injured by the shot from the English ships when they bombarded Genoa about 5 years since. When we arrived at *Sestri di Ponenti* we stopped to visit at the house of Mrs Bird lady of the English consul. She resides at a little distance from Sestri, the house being charmingly situated on a small eminence on the sea shore. I was here introduced to Mrs Bird and her daughters—and to a M^rs^ W—— & her daughters who are on a visit of some weeks at Mrs Birds. The girls were very lively and agreeable. The eldest Miss Bird to the graces of a fine person and beautiful countenance adds the accomplishments of an excellent English education and the attractions of an amiable disposition. The sister Eliza has a goodneſs of heart and mildneſs of manner that cannot fail to engage esteem and tho the small pox has unfortunately destroyed her pretensions to beauty yet it could not deprive her of that good nature that shines in her countenance. The younger sister Harriet is yet quite young but promises to poſseſs the highest accomplishments of mind and person. The daughters of M^rs^ W—— are not very remarkable either in person or manner. As to their mother she is one of those *knowing*, *notable* kind of women. Has read considerable and sets up for a *woman of learning*— a dangerous character for a woman to sustain who has not strength of head or delicacy of face & judgement sufficient to support it. Mrs Bird is a charming woman. Polite without ceremony — attentive and hospitable without being officious and poſseſsed of good sense without the ostentation of it.

Understanding we had come out of town on a

ramble she prefsed us to return there to dinner to which we consented, having obtaind the consent of the young ladies to accompany us in our visit to the Lomellino garden at Pali. This garden is as I before said, laid out in the English taste and deserves a visit from the traveller who stays any time at Genoa. It has a variety of fine walks, Groves, grottos, rivulets, a hermitage, a rustic theatre, a temple &c &c &c and delightful glimpses are caught of the Medditerranean from different parts of the Garden. The Society of the ladies rendered our ramble delightful & we did not find our way-back to the house till three oclock. Before dinner the ladies entertained us with playing on the Harpsichord and singing in both which they acquitted themselves very handsomely. The dinner hour pafsed away very merrily, we were all in high spirits and as soon as we left the table we began to dance to the music of the Harpsichord. It was not till late in the evening that Storm & myself reccollected that we were engaged at Lady Shaftsesburys and that we had no time to lose in getting to town. We parted therefore from the ladies with infinite reluctance and set out on our return.

The night was dark and rainy and when we arrived at St Pietra d' Arena we found that the city gates was shut and no carriage would be admitted.

It rained too hard to think of returning home from the gates on foot as the distance was very far, so we stopped in the little theatre of S[t] Pietra till the rain should subside.

The theatre was a miserable little hole and the performance very poor. One of the Actrefses, a very pretty girl, happened to be an old *acquaintance* of Storms and in the course of the play when she had fainted away and was reclining in a most pathetic situation in an arm chair—Storm pelted her with balls of paper. This had nearly involved us in a quarrel with a couple of French officers—however, after a few words they thought proper to keep themselves silent. After remaining here an hour the rain ceased and we set out again on our journey homeward, where we arrived after having waded thro mud holes and encountered various accidents *by flood & field.* It was too late to think of going to Lady Shaftesburys that evening so we went to bed highly satisfied with our days amusement.

[*October*] 27th

Yesterday evening I was introduced by Storm to Lord & Lady Shaftesbury. His Lordship & family are detained here prisoners of war having been arrested above a year ago while on their travels. He is one of the richest earls of England his income being 40,000£ sterling a year. His lordship received a violent injury on the head by a fall from his horse some years since which produced a derangement of intellect for some time. He has never perfectly recovered from the effects of it, exhibiting continually an excentricity in his conversation and manners. He often makes some extravagant observation and exprefses his ideas a little wildly. He appears to pofsefs a very good disposition is extremely polite and evinces a continual fear of offending. At the end of almost every remark he makes he seizes you by the hand and exclaims—"My dear sir—I hope I have not offended you—I may be very wrong in my opinion—but I have not offended you, have I? you'll excuse me, I cannot be certain—but I think—I believe I am not very wrong but I havn't given offence—now—have I?" And this whimsical string of exprefsions is often made after the most trifling & indifferent observation staring you earnestly in the face & rubbing his forehead with one hand all the while.

His Lordship exprefses great friendship for the Americans and together with his lady thinks we are advancing rapidly to become the first nation in the world.

Lady Shaftesbury is an affable, charming woman

—and still bears the remains of great beauty. She sets you at ease immediately in her presence releasing you from all painful ceremoniousnefs of manner by her sociability. She plays charmingly on the piano and Harp and never requires a second request to play if she is really in a humor for music. They have with them their only child Lady Barbara Ashley Cooper a very pretty girl of about fifteen, extremely lively. Great care is taken to instruct her in all the fashionable accomplishments. She talks French & Italian fluently, plays on the piano, harp & Guitar and is very good humord.

Our reception was very polite and satisfactory Storm being an old acquaintance and favorite of her Ladyship.

November 8th [1804]

SINCE writing last, the time has pafsed very pleasantly away, having been introduced by Storm to some of the first Nobility of Genoa. Taken collectively, I cannot speak very highly in praise of them. They seem to be a stupid set of beings without much talent or information. The deprefsed state of their country and the misfortunes they have undergone may have deprefsed their spirits and produced a change in their manners, tho' as far as I can find from different authors they never were celebrated for much wit & learning. Some among them however are very agreeable—many of them speak English & almost all of them French so that I have no difficulty in conversing with them.

We have been out two or three times since to Sestri, and rambled about its romantic environs accompanied by the ladies. We have dined once since with M[rs] Bird and met at her house a M[r] Alton a Swifs Gentleman who talks English perfectly and a M[r] Wilson a Scotch painter who pafses for an American and has been above a year in Genoa purchasing paintings &c. The former is an old Batchelor that still retains all his boyish waggery and is very fond of *fun*, the latter a good natured good kind of a fellow & a true *sawney*. Our evenings at Sestri were generally spent in dancing or playing games of sport and delighted me from the resemblance they bore to the pleasant ones I have pafsed among my female acquaintances in America. As to Storm and myself we were so delighted with the place and its fair inhabitants that we generally slept at the hotel in the town all night & did not get home till late the next day. The sober Italians stare at us often with surprize and call us the *wild Americans*. They generally remark that the Americans and English are just alike except that the Americans are wilder & have a higher flow of spirits.

Yesterday we paid a Visit to Madame Gabriac, a lady of distinction to whom I was introduced some time since. Here we found a Signor Moranda an Italian gentelman of Storms acquaintance who speaks English fluently. He proposed that we should accompany him to the country seat of Madame Brignoli at Voltri about ten miles to the west of Genoa on the Sea Shore. Madame Brignoli has a *Dillitanti theatre* at her country seat and they were to perform Voltaires tragedy of Zaira that evening. We agreed to accompany him in the afternoon. We sat off about four oclock being accommodated with seats in the carriage of Madame Genestons sister in law to madame Gabriac. This lady was one of the maids of Honor to the late Queen of France and was a witneſs to many of the scenes of Blood that took place in Paris at the commencement of the revolution. She was present in the room when the head of Madame Lamballe was struck off by the sanguinary mob. The horrid scene had such an effect on her mind as to produce a derangement of intellect from which she was a long time recovering.

It has subsided into a melancholy that has become habitual & settled. We arrived at the palace of Madame Brignoli some time after dark. I was introduced to her and had an extremely polite reception. She is a woman of a fine person & features and elegant manner and is said to be one of the most intelligent ladies of Genoa. She is one of the richest members of the Brignoli family — (a family of the highest rank in the Genoese republic). We found here a number of the beau monde of Genoa amusing themselves with billiards till the play commenced. After paſsing about an hour in the billiard room we were summoned to the theatre. This is fitted up with taste & judgment & great expence in one wing of the palace. A place in front of the Stage in what we call the pit is seperated from the other part of the theatre for the reception of Madame Brignoli's visitors. The rest of the theatre consisting of the back part of the pit and a gallery is free for the country people. Zaira the heroine of the play was performed by Madame Reverolle and was her first attempt at theatrics. She is a lady of much beauty and acquitted herself remarkably well. The hero was represented by the eldest son of Madam Brignoli about 18 years old—tall and well made. His performance was energetic & graceful—his voice, tho hardly of sufficient strength & flexibility was however full & manly. As the language of the play was Italian I could not judge how he succeeded in the dialogue, but he appeared to give much satisfaction to the audience. The other characters were sustaind tolerably well — Madame

Brignoli filld one of the female characters but had not scope to display her dramatic powers. After the play we partook of an elegant supper furnished in a room that was decorated to represent a Grotto.

The walls were inlaid with porcelaine in imitation of scales & shells and marine productions were distributed with great taste. The *tout ensemble* was superb and must have required a vast expence. After supper word was brought us that the rain that had fallen in great quantities all the evening together with the floods from the mountains had swelld a small river, which we had to crofs on our way to town, to such a degree as to render it very dangerous to pafs it in the dark. We were therefore obliged to remain at Madam Brignoli's till morning. To pafs away the time we adjourned to another room and danced, between the dances some ladies & gentlemen performed on different instruments & sung. Lady Shaftesbury & Lady Barbara were present the latter was in high spirits & danced with great vivacity. In spight of every endeavor we began to be fatigued & heavy before daylight. Storm fell asleep on a sofa having in vain endeavored to persuade a young lady to let him lay his head in her lap. At length the morning dawnd and we sat off for home as weary a looking set as ever was seen at the breaking up of a ball. We nodded to one another very sociably the whole ride and once or twice a jolt of the carriage sent all our sleepy heads together.

[*November*] 13th

Yesterday Storm & myself rode out to Sestri to Mrs Birds with an intention of rambling upon the mountains. We had not been there long before we were joind by Mr Wilson whom the fine weather had likewise induced to visit the country. The ladies consented to accompany us in clambering up the heights, and to shew us such places as commanded the most beautiful prospects. The ascent of the mountains was steep & rugged but we were amply repaid by the variety of views that continually opened upon us. The deep gullies between the mountains were well cultivated and cottages appeared on every side, and thro the mountain vistas we caught fine glimpses of the sea shore and the Village of Sestri. From one of the highest places we could see Genoa in the distance—its steeples & towers having a very picturesque effect on the landscape. On the other side a long stretch of the sea shore with villages palaces &c and behind, the Appenines gradually rising up in vast rocky heights. While we were at this spot enjoying the charming prospects we were surprized by the sound of some uncouth instrument and looking round we perceived a strange, ragged figure approaching us. He was short & brown, his clothes of the rainbow order and an old woolen cap on his head. His countenance was sturdy and good humord and his black eyes had a peculiar archneſs of expreſsion. His instrument was a simple piece of reed with three slits that ran half its length and by blowing on this and humoring the reed with his hand he produced sufficient variety of notes to perform a few simple rustic airs.

He advanced towards us with his cap under his arm, played two or three of his tunes and then handed us very goodhumordly his instrument to examine. We gave him a few sous tho he had not requested them. He did not make any acknowledgements but laughed & appeard mightily pleased. While we were looking at him and his reed he very quietly took some mushrooms out of his cap & began to eat them raw. He told the ladies his name and said he knew where they lived and would come to their palace and play on his reed under their windows. We afterwards learned from some peasants that he was foolish but a harmleſs inofensive good humord fellow that rambled about in the neighborhood of Sestri and was supported by the peasants.

Advancing a little farther up the mountain we

stopped at a peasants cottage built of Stone in form of a Square tower and half embowrd in large chestnut trees and of a picturesque appearance. Here the ladies told us they had taken shelter one day when a shower of rain had surprized them in one of their rambles and they had been so much delighted with the inhabitants of the cottage as to be induced often to visit them. The family consisted of an old man & his wife, a healthy contented looking couple, three daughters & two sons. The girls were the handsomest female peasants that I have seen in Italy —or I may say in Europe. One in particular, had a blooming complexion, fine black eyes a beautiful set of teethe and when she smiled, two of the prettiest dimples imaginable. Tho drefsd in the coarse rustic manner, there was a neatnefs & cleanlinefs about her, seldom to be found among the peasantry excepting on Sundays & hollidays. Her name accorded with her person, and was one of those that we denominate *romantic* tho one by no means uncommon in Italy—it was Angelina (I E *little angel*). The inhabitants of the cottage crowded around us seeming much pleased with our visit and delighted to see the ladies. After stopping a little while we sat out to ascend higher and the pretty Angelina offerd to accompany us, to guide us to a very pleasant spot.

The place where she led us was a little plain that formd a kind of terrace on the top of one of the heights and commanded the most enchanting views on every side. We remained here a long time before we were satisfied with looking about us, and Angelina employed herself in the meantime in gathering flowers for us. We asked her a great many questions to which she answered with much simplicity and good humor. Tho within six miles of Genoa she had only been there but twice in her life tho she was now eighteen years old. She had all the artleſsneſs of nature and amused us much with her replies. Mr Wilson asked her if she had not any sweetheart yet. She replied without hesitation "That she loved Iacimo, and that Iacimo loved her likewise and they were to be married in about a year." We asked her who Iacimo was and she told us he was a young man that lived in Sestri, and that he came to see her very often and that she always saw him when she went to church on Sundays at Sestri — that he was a charming young man — a very charming young man (Uno Amabilleſsimo Giovinotto).

She appeared to be quite unreserved in her replies, tho she blushed and smild whenever she was talking of Iacimo. We returned to the cottage to dispatch a loaf of bread which we had brought with us. The good people were very eager to serve us.

They handed us benches immediately and produced a pitcher of milk for us to eat with our bread. Good humor and content seemed to reign in this happy family and for the first time I realized in Europe the many poetic pictures I have read of rustic felicity.

Our return down the mountain was by a different route which likewise abounded with beautiful scenery.

The rest of the day & the evening paſsed away very pleasantly with the ladies whose society was of that easy unaffected kind that banishes all disagreeable ceremonious restraint. The house of Mrs Bird, commands an extensive and variegated view. A terrace, particularly on one wing overlooks a charming prospect. The sea shore and the village of Sestri built along it, at a distance the Suburbs of St Pietra d'Arena beyond which rises the ridge of mountains on which is built the wall of Genoa running into the sea and terminated with the high tower or light house. The whole shore and the skirts of the mountains, from the village of Sestri to Genoa, is a succeſsion of villages palaces &c interspersed with delightful gardens, behind the Appinines rear their rocky summits. On the other hand is the vast bosom of the Middeterranean — speckled with sails of veſsels, feluccas, fishing boats paſsing & repaſsing continually — and in another direction is seen the

Genoese coast stretching as far as the eye can see, forming a continued chain of rocky Mountains at the feet of which the white villages & chateaus brighten in the sun. And between the intervalls of the grey summits of the Appinines you catch glimpses of the Alps at a great distance, covered with eternal snow and shining with reflection of the Sun beams. The whole surrounding scenery is of the richest & most charming variety and at sunrise or sunset, is really enchanting.

[*November*] 14th

Yesterday we were invited to Mrs Birds to eat *Ravioli* and spend the day. Ravioli is a favorite Genoese dish made of flour and forced meat and is very delicate. Yesterday was the day of St Martins when it is universally eaten by the Genoese the same as [*blank*] is on Good friday by the English. They generally invite several of their friends to dine with them & make merry and after that day the fashionable world commonly abandon their country residences and return to town. The lower claſses make it a point to get drunk on the occasion and will often compel persons to do so who are soberly inclined. The day & evening paſsed away very agreeably the latter as usual being devoted to dancing. We returned to town early this morning.

At eleven oclock today, took place the execution of a notorious robber who has for some time made a great noise in Europe and was known by the name of *The Great Devil of Genoa* (Il grand Diavolo).

The real name of this man was Joseph Mufso— he was born in Genoa, of obscure parentage and followed the occupations of a common laborer or peasant till the time the Germans beseiged Genoa. He then enlisted under the German Standard and by his bravery acquired some inferior commifsion. When the German Army withdrew from the country he remained behind but being outlawed he did not dare to appear in his native city. His military life had innured him to toils & dangers and gave a warlike turn to his disposition. His fortunes were desperate, he had sworn eternal enmity to the French & Bonaparte in particular—the whole country was in the hands of his enemies and he could expect no mercy at their hands. Every door to honest subsistence being thus shut against him he determined to have resort to robbery for a livelihood and violate those laws which had already sat their faces against him. He soon found companions equally desperate with himself and formed a band that in a short time became notorious and dreaded for its intrepid exploits. The Appinines in the neighborhood of Genoa afforded safe retreats for his band from whence they frequently descended to lay travellers under contribution and plunder convoys of merchandize. But their depredations were not entirely confined to these parts—They extended to other parts of Italy and even it is supposed he was often a leader in many signal robberies in Spain.

A favorite scene of his crimes was at the Boquetto a rugged paſs over a mountain on the road to Milan. It is the only paſs by which a carriage can enter or leave the Ligurian republick & is consequently much travelled. Here from the steepneſs & roughneſs of the mountain it was impoſsible for either carriage or horseman to escape from his gang—and robberies were inceſsant in this spot. His band seldom consisted of above eighteen or twenty—but they were all men of desperate courage & their mode of life had innured them to hardships & fatigue. The name of *The Great Devil* (given him in consequence of his incredible exploits) soon became universally dreaded. Troops of soldiers were sent out to take or destroy him but he invariably escaped from their toils. At one time they surrounded him & his comrades on the top of a mountain, but they cut thro their enemies & effected their escape. His bodily strength was astonishing & he was equally remarkable for his agility in running,—bounding among the rocks & precipices of the mountains like a goat. Another time a company of soldiers surrounded a small hut in which he was sleeping, he leapd out of a window, fought his way thro them & got off unhurt though a volley of musketry was fired at him. There was a considerable degree of discrimination observed by him in his robberies. He never plundered the poor, but often relieved them by the spoils he had taken from the rich. The poor peasants frequently experienced the effects of his bounty and he was careful to cultivate a good understanding with all the peasantry in his neighborhood. He was therefore very secure from being betrayed by them even when they knew his lurking place and large rewards were offered for his apprehension. His relations & friends in Genoa gave him notice of everything that was carrying on so that he knew when to profit by convoys of merchandize or to escape parties that were sent out in pursuit of him. At one time when a body of soldiers were searching for him in the mountains he was sailing off the harbor in a small boat. Another time an officer of police was sent to insinuate himself into his band & act as a spy. He repaired to the Great Devil & offered his services as a man who was unfortunate and ill treated by the world—Mufso who had information of his intentions turned to some of his gang who was present & orderd them to lead forth that man and shoot him—the orders were immediately obeyd.

Any persons that wished to trade with him for his spoils might rely on his *honor* and safely bring any sum of money to purchase them with. The Great Devil had plunderd a rich convoy of Goods belonging to a merch[t] of Genoa. The latter sent his brother to treat for their redemption. Mufso gave him a meeting—having his guards stationd at a little distance to prevent surprize. The Merch[t] offerd him a price very much inferior to the value of the goods—Mufso replied "do you think your brother would have sold them at such a miserable rate!—They have become mine by capture and I cannot think of sacrificing my goods at so inferior a price." The merch[t] pafsed the night in Mufso's tent; in consequence of his afsurance of safety—in the morning he took leave unmolested altho' he had a large sum of gold by him to make the purchase—he afterwards returned with the sum Mufso required. It would be tiresome to enter into a detail of his manouvres and the many accounts I have heard of his different exploits for several years. His robberies & murders had been transacted in different parts of Italy, Germany, France, Spain & Portugal and he has been condemned to death & prices set on his head by different courts in those different territories. After the many regular attempts to apprehend him, the busineſs was effected by a Mere Accident. He had taken paſsage from Gibraltar in a veſsel bound to Trieste a port in Germany to the eastward of Venice. While performing Quarentine at Trieste he had a violent Quarrel with the Master & swore that the latter should not live long after they were landed.

Intimidated by this menace and by the manner of the person who made it the captain as soon as he landed applied to the proper authorities for protection — mentioning that a Genoese on board of his veſsel threatened his life. The Magistrate applied to the Genoese consul to become responsible for Muſso. The consul was struck with the name and immediately suspected from the discription given that it might be the notorious robber of whom in common with all Genoese authorities—he had been put on his guard. He went on board of the Veſsel and was confirmed in the opinion. He instantly had him apprehended & thrown in prison & wrote to Genoa an account of the affair. A company of soldiers were immediately dispatched who brought him to Genoa where he was closely confined in the Tower. After an imprisonment of three months he was convicted & sentenced to be shot. He was brought to the chapel of the prison to have the sentence read to him by a Priest. A gentleman of my acquaintance was at the prison at the time & mentioned to me the particulars. It was Friday evening. Mufso came skipping down stairs between two soldiers—with a carelefs air smoking a pipe & jumping two steps at a time. When the priest read off the sentence he showed no signs of agitation but replied carelefsly "è *bene* (very well)—you might as well have sentenced me at first and not kept me three months in prison."

He was then going off but stopped and turning briskly round—"Stop says he—you have forgot to tell me when I am to be shot" The priest replied "on *Monday*"—"Saturday is *one*, Sunday *two*, Monday *three* (replied he counting his fingers) three days—è *bene*" and was then again going off very unconcernedly but added "I suppose I may see my sister & relations before I am shot" he was told that could not be granted "then replied he they will have to drag me to execution for my own feet shall not carry me there." He was then led to the dungeon where the condemned are confined between the reading & execution of their sentence. He was allowed to see his relations the next day and Sunday—being S[t] Martins when all the Genoese eat raviolis, a dish of the kind cooked in the best manner, was given him & they searched Genoa for a bottle of the finest wine (a bottle of good wine is always given to the condemned in Genoa before execution) which was furnished by an old princefs of my acquaintance. This morning all Genoa was in commotion (I E the lower class) to see him shot. As the Police was apprehensive an attempt might be made to rescue him by his relations & the peasantry (the latter being highly prepofsefsed in his favor from the liberality with which he had often distributed his plunder among them) a large body of soldiers were ordered out to guard him to the place of execution.

The streets — windows &c were throngd by spectators. Having in common with the multitude a great curiosity to see this singular man I stationed myself at the gate of the city at which he was to go out — & had a tolerable view of him as he pafsed. He appeard to be about five feet 8 inches, stout & well set, of a dark complexion with strong but good features & immence eyebrows. He was about 26 years of age.

Two priests attended him to whom he appeared to listen very devoutly and he held a small crofs between his hands. He was shot on the banks of a small river that runs without the town, and sufferd his sentence in a very manly decent manner. I have been particular in my account of this man from his great celebrity. An account was published some time ago in England of his apprehension & execution—and an Afterpiece written of which he was the hero. In a better cause he might have distinguished himself to advantage—he certainly posseſsed superior genius & undaunted courage.

[*November*] 16th

Yesterday we dined at Lord Shaftesbury's. There were but three or four visitors at table beside ourselves, but after dinner in the evening more company came in and violins having been prepared we had a pleasant little dance. The Italians do not equal the French in dancing altho' they have dancing Masters of that nation. As there are not many Gentlemen among the Nobility who excel in dancing, they are obliged when they give balls to invite merchants clerks, to aſsist in making up the dances —these they call "the dancers of the city" & are considered much in the light of joint stools or arm chairs sometimes used in family dances to make up a set for a cotillion or country dance. Ices & lemonades are handed about at the balls continually—and the Italians make no hesitation in eating the former when in a state of the highest perspiration.

NOTES ON THE TEXT OF VOLUME I

NOTES ON THE TEXT

OF VOLUME I

PAGE 6, LINES 18, 19: *This injures the looks of their edifices*

injures

The manuscript reads: "~~This gives a disa diminishes,~~" showing that the writer made two unsuccessful attempts before finding a satisfactory expression. The *Journal* has numerous corrections and changes of this nature; only the most important are noted.

PAGE 7, LINE 11: *a Gentleman of taste arrived from Paris*

Probably the politician and biographer of Napoleon, Comte Antoine Claire Thibaudeau, appointed prefect of the Gironde by Napoleon in 1800. As President of the Convention, he had occupied himself chiefly with educational matters, notably in the organization of the Museum of the Louvre, so that his interest in the preservation of so precious a "remain of antiquity" as the Palais Gallien is not surprising.

PAGE 8, LINE 9: *The Grand Theatre is a magnificent building*

Built by Victor Louis in 1773–80 at the expense of the town, it still holds its rank as one of the finest theatres in Europe, the staircase, of which Irving first wrote "magnificent," correcting it to "superb," being one of its most noticeable features.

PAGE 8, LINE 21: *I have been twice to see La Fond*

Pierre Lafon began his studies for the stage in Bordeaux at the age of sixteen, and his tragedy, *La Mort d'Hercule*, was performed there two years later, in 1793. He died in Bordeaux in 1846.

PAGE 9, LINE 18: *the Emperor and his conduct.*
Bordeaux never reconciled itself to the rule of Napoleon, who seriously injured its commerce. He had been proclaimed Emperor on May 18, less than six weeks before Irving's arrival in France, although the coronation by the Pope did not take place until December 2, when Irving was at Genoa. (*See his allusion, Vol. II, p.* 9.)

PAGE 13, LINES 12–26: *Amid all the scenes . . . interests.*
These lines as well as lines 4–11 on p. 17 and lines 8–11 on p. 18 are in a different ink from that of the Bordeaux entries and seem to have been written in the blank spaces left in the *Journal* after the traveller reached Toulouse, when he used the blue ink of these additions. There are several cases of such careful additions throughout the *Journal*.

PAGE 14, LINE 11: *the words of Congreve*
Irving at first wrote: "the words of our immortal bard," and the first line of the quotation from Congreve's *Mourning Bride* (Act II, Scene 1), adding "&c." Later, in a different ink, he supplied the remainder of the passage, with the poet's name, crossing out "our immortal bard."

PAGE 20, LINES 23, 24: *The spire . . . was blown down*
The hurricane which destroyed the spire of the bell

tower of St. Michel (standing about one hundred feet from the church) occurred in 1768. The spire was not rebuilt until 1861–69.

PAGE 22, LINE 7: *in favor of the American girls.*
Below this entry the author made several unsuccessful attempts to describe the manner of walking of the French: "~~The In walking the fr~~ I am ~~In walking the~~"

PAGE 24, LINE 25: *Dibdin's "Tom Bowling."*
Charles Dibdin's popular sea song was inspired by the Lieutenant Tom Bowling of Smollett's *Roderick Random.*

PAGE 38, LINES 1–12: *In this place . . . criticise*
This description of Dr. Henry forms the first quotation from the *Journal* used by Pierre Irving in his *Life and Letters of Washington Irving.*

PAGE 39, LINE 4: *At Tonneins as we were patroling*
Pierre Irving quotes a letter to Washington's brother, William, narrating the Tonneins incident, and another to his sister, describing his second visit in 1845 when, on his way from Madrid to Paris, as American Minister to Spain, he shaped his course so as to revisit Tonneins.

PAGE 52, LINE 15, TO PAGE 53, LINE 2: *In one town . . . breakfast.*
Compare *Life and Letters,* where this is quoted as from a letter to his brother William. Irving often copied from the *Journal* in writing home.

PAGE 53, LINES 16–20: *one of whom . . . vagabond.*
Pierre Irving quotes this incident as an example of the author's "nervous impetuosity under annoyance"

PAGE 55, LINE 11: *about the size of our theatre*
The writer was probably referring to the John Street Theatre, and perhaps remembering his boyish escapades when he visited it by way of his window and the back roofs. A flourishing rival of the John Street Theatre was the Old Park, opened in 1798.

PAGE 61, LINE 8: *the houses still stand there*
The Amphitheatre of Nîmes was finally freed from hovels in 1809.

PAGE 62, LINE 13, TO PAGE 63, LINE 2: *By some conversation . . . lightly.*
Quoted in *Life and Letters*, where the two passports are described. Concerning the varying descriptions of the eyes (blue and brown), Pierre Irving writes: "Their actual color was sometimes a moot point among his friends."

PAGE 65, LINES 24, 25: *the Church de Notre Dame de Don*
The Cathedral of Notre Dame des Doms.

PAGE 66, LINES 23, 24: *For seventy two years this was the seat of the popes*
Avignon had been chosen for his residence by Clement V in 1309, and the papal see was restored to Italy by Gregory XI in 1377, so that Irving is slightly mistaken in his computation of seventy-two years.

PAGE 73, LINES 6–19: *I was agreeably surprized . . . cricket.*
Quoted in *Life and Letters.*

PAGE 75, LINE 22: *Blanchard (the Aereal navigator . . .)*
If this were Jean Pierre Blanchard, Irving saw the first man who had crossed the English Channel in the air. For this achievement he was accorded distinguished honors at Versailles, from the King, the Royal Family, the Minister, and other great officers of the State. Some years later he came to America, and on January 9, 1793, made the first balloon ascension accomplished in this country. It took place at Philadelphia, and George Washington, then President of the United States, who had already received M. Blanchard, was a witness of the event.

PAGE 76, LINE 6: *Yorick relates . . . Strafsburg*
The reference is to *Slawkenbergius's Tale* in Sterne's *Tristram Shandy*, Vol. IV.

PAGE 77, LINE 8: *talks English fluently.*
Following this, two passages are blotted out in the *Journal*, and a leaf is cut out.

PAGE 80, LINE 8: *(vide Ferg. Rom. Rep.)*
Adam Ferguson's *History of the Progress and Termination of the Roman Republic* appeared in 1782, and seems to have been a favorite authority with Irving. Carlyle, in his rectorial address to the students of Edinburgh University, where Ferguson was pro-

fessor of philosophy, spoke of him as "particularly well worth reading in Roman history."

PAGE 83, LINE 5, TO PAGE 84, LINE 1: *Fortunately . . . enough for me."*

The following letter to William Irving, quoted in the *Life and Letters*, shows how Irving used the *Journal* as a basis for his letters home: "Fortunately for me, I am seasoned, in some degree, to the disagreeables from my Canada journey of last summer. When I enter one of these inns, to put up for the night, I have but to draw a comparison between it and some of the log hovels into which my fellow-travellers and myself were huddled, after a fatiguing day's journey through the woods, and the inn appears a palace. For my part I endeavor to take things as they come, with cheerfulness, and when I cannot get a dinner to suit my taste, I endeavor to get a taste to suit my dinner . . . There is nothing I dread more than to be taken for one of the Smellfungii of this world. I therefore endeavor to be pleased with everything about me, and with the masters, mistresses, and servants of the inns, particularly when I perceive they have 'all the dispositions in the world,' to serve me; as Sterne says, 'It is enough for heaven and ought to be enough for me.'" Irving's journey to Ogdensburg, Montreal, and Quebec was made at the invitation of Josiah Ogden Hoffman in the summer of 1803.

PAGE 83, LINE 22: *one of the Smellfungii*

Smollett was ridiculed by Sterne, in *A Sentimental Journey*, under the name "Smelfungus," because of the perpetual fault finding in his *Travels through France and Italy*. The two quotations are from the *Sentimental Journey* (*In the Street.—Montreuil*).

PAGE 86, LINE 22: *to choose our rooms immediately.*
The following has been crossed out, after "immediately:" "This precaution was well timed for just before supper the hostess came in with a countenance somewhat perplexed and told us that the Engineer general of the Department had just arrived with his lady—that he was *un grand homme* and ought to be well accommodated—that he patronized her inn and wished to have my room as it was the best in the inn—that therefore she." The last nine words are not included in the crossing out, but are followed by about a dozen lines, which have been rendered illegible.

PAGE 87, LINES 13–15: *Bonaparte & his suite . . . Quarantine*
Napoleon disembarked at Fréjus on October 9, 1799, after a perilous voyage from Alexandria. The failure to "perform quarantine" is said to have been due to the enthusiasm of the populace, who so crowded into the vessels as to render it impracticable.

PAGE 90, LINE 27: *the little village of Cannes*
At the time of Irving's visit, Cannes was a mere fishing village. The residence of Lord Brougham, who took much interest in the place and died there in 1868, founded its reputation as a winter resort.

PAGE 93, LINE 15: *to a friend & to our Consul*
The letter to William (quoted above) shows that the

friend referred to was Dr. Ellison, at whose recommendation the writer had been admitted into the Ferrier household at Bordeaux, and that the American Consul was Mr. Lee.

PAGE 93, LINE 20: *my friend S——*
"Hall Storm, here mentioned, was a native of New York, established in business at Genoa, and then acting as vice-consul. He had been an early playmate of Mr. Irving, though somewhat his senior." (*Life and Letters.*)

PAGE 94, LINE 10: *voice like that of Tom Pipes*
Tom Pipes is the retired boatswain's mate of Smollett's *Peregrine Pickle.*

PAGE 102, LINE 8: *the offer of my Uncle Toby*
"'You shall go home directly, Le Fevre, said my uncle Toby, to my house,— and we 'll send for a doctor to see what 's the matter; — and we 'll have an apothecary; — and the Corporal shall be your nurse: and I 'll be your servant, Le Fevre.'" (Sterne. *Tristram Shandy*, Vol. VI.)

PAGE 108, LINES 2, 3: *Robt L Livingston Esqr Son in law of the Minister*
Robert L. Livingston, a kinsman of Chancellor Robert R. Livingston, American minister to France, 1801–5, had married the Chancellor's daughter, and accompanied his father-in-law to France as private secretary.

PAGE 109, LINE 4 : *Mr Lowel an American gentleman*

Through the courtesy of Miss Amy Lowell, we learn that this Mr. Lowell was her great-grandfather, John, brother of James Russell Lowell's father. Retiring from the practice of law in 1803, at the age of thirty-four, Mr. John Lowell travelled for three years in Europe with his wife, who was a Miss Amory, and his sister, Miss Anna Cabot Lowell. On his return from Europe he devoted himself to botany and horticulture, and wrote many political articles for the newspapers.

PAGE 118, LINES 1–5, *and* PAGE 119, LINES 12–25 : *Our Padrone . . . heads* and *The breeze . . . Ave Maria.*

Although in the *Life and Letters* the *Journal* is said to be quoted here, there is much dissimilarity.

PAGE 121, LINE 4 : *Cocorato*

Probably Cogoleto, said to be the birthplace of Columbus.

PAGE 122, LINE 23 : *I called upon S——*

In describing Irving's warm welcome from his friend, Storm, Pierre Irving writes, "with whom he took up his quarters in the wing of an old palace." He also quotes from a letter to William : "I cannot speak with sufficient warmth of the reception I have met with from Storm. We have scarcely been out of each other's sight all the time I have been here, and he has introduced me to the first society in Genoa, from whom I have received the most flattering attentions."

PAGE 125, LINE 9: *an Emerald dish*
The *Sacro Catino*, captured by the Genoese at Caesarea in 1101, was supposed to be made of a large emerald until broken on being sent to Paris by Napoleon, when it was discovered to be only a remarkable piece of ancient glass. It was returned to Genoa in fragments, and mended by a goldsmith there.

PAGE 129, LINE 18: *would be very inconsiderable*
After this, Irving wrote and crossed out "as those who have boxes are admitted free the same as at other times."

PAGE 132, LINE 4: *Pali.*
Pegli.

PAGE 133, LINE 24, *and* PAGE 135, LINE 7: *Lord & Lady Shaftesbury. . . . their only child Lady Barbara*
Anthony, fifth Earl of Shaftesbury, married in 1786 Barbara, daughter and heiress of Sir John Week. Their daughter, Barbara, married in 1814 the Hon. William Ponsonby, created Lord de Manley in 1838. She died in 1844.

PAGE 136, LINE 10: *Mr Wilson a Scotch painter*
Andrew Wilson, the landscape painter, born in Edinburgh in 1780. In 1803, he visited Italy for the second time, settling at Genoa, and was made a member of the Ligurian Academy. At Genoa he was occupied chiefly in purchasing pictures of the old masters, of which he obtained no less than fifty-four.

PAGE 137, LINES 14, 15 : *one of the maids of Honor to the late Queen*

The Countess Ginestons was lady-in-waiting to the Princess de Lamballe, and remained in Paris during the Revolution with the hope of assisting the Princess and the Queen. She afterward retired to England and was supposed to have lost her mind.

PAGE 153, LINE 3: *an Afterpiece written*

Probably *The Great Devil: or, The Robber of Genoa. By Charles Dibdin, jun. Acted at Sadlers' Wells,* 1801, which ends with the death of the bandit, thus anticipating the event by several years. The short play appeared again in Cumberland's *Minor Theatre*, Vol. XIV, 1832, when George Daniel wrote, in his *Introduction:* "We remember with the freshness of yesterday the sensations it produced; every faculty was absorbed in sight and hearing: terror, wonder and amazement rapidly succeeded . . . The Great Devil is understood to have been a real character, who, with thirty robbers as ferocious as himself, outdid all former desperadoes."